THE CENTRAL SCHOOL OF SPEECH AND DRAMA

UNIVERSITY OF LONDON

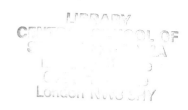
STREET DREAMS

AMERICAN CAR CULTURE
FROM THE FIFTIES TO THE EIGHTIES

DAVID BARRY

Macdonald Orbis

This book is dedicated to my wife, Kanthi Kathleen

A Macdonald Orbis BOOK

© Macdonald & Co (Publishers) Ltd

First published in Great Britain in 1988
by Macdonald & Co (Publishers) Ltd
London & Sydney

A member of Maxwell Pergamon Publishing Corporation plc

British Library Cataloguing in Publication Data

Barry, David
    Street dreams
    1. United States. Cars. 1950–1987
    1. Title
    629.2'222'0973

    ISBN 0–356–15569–2

Typeset by Q-Set, Hucclecote, Gloucester
Printed and bound in Great Britain by Purnell Book Production,
a member of BPCC plc

Editor: Jennifer Jones
Art Director: Linda Cole
Designer: Alan Gooch
Indexer: Alex Corrin

Macdonald & Co (Publishers) Ltd
Greater London House
Hampstead Road
London NW1 7QX

CONTENTS

INTRODUCTION

Songwriter Bobby Troupe probably said it best in the classic hit *Route 66* written right after World War II on a cross-country auto trip with his wife. Inspired by a road sign for the two-lane highway across the wide-open spaces from Chicago to Los Angeles, the song *Route 66* conjured up an image of a fast car, a convertible with the top down for romance, excitement and adventure on the way to California. The song told only of the road itself, the cities and the states it went through on the 2000-mile journey, but that was enough to fuel the dreams of millions who might never drive it except in their minds and fantasies. The song celebrates the highway, which is part of the passionate American affair with the car, a love affair that shapes the American landscape, defines the way Americans travel and says a great deal about what Americans think of themselves.

Like no other society, twentieth-century America has grown up with the automobile. In Britain, France, Germany and the rest of Europe, cars were conveyances for the privileged until after World War II; autos only came into widespread use in the sixties or seventies. But cars were already woven into the tapestry of American dreams before World War I, and by the twenties they were a common sight throughout the

United States. Just as the horse, the cowboy and the pioneer represented a rugged, wandering spirit native to America, the automobile fulfilled a fundamental American desire for freedom, power and mobility. Because cars were made in such large numbers and at such low prices, anyone who held a job could afford one from the time of the Model A Ford onwards. Competition soon produced cars that offered much more than a basic means of transport; cars became recreation vehicles in America a generation or more before they were widely used for basic transportation in other countries.

Of course, the American taste for big, stylish, fast cars was never unique. In Germany, Spain, Italy, Britain and France the same qualities were admired and desired. But in Europe only the privileged few could indulge such dreams. In America, from early in the twentieth century, a flashy, sporty car was something almost any working man could buy, and it was part of almost everyone's dream.

After World War II, dream cars were bigger, more exciting and more desirable than ever to a population enjoying prosperity on a wider scale than ever before. From the fifties onwards, a dream car was no longer a private passion, an unattainable object of desire, but something to own and drive. If a brand-new Chevy or Ford or Plymouth was too expensive on the instalment plan, a used one could be purchased for $5 down and $5 a week.

There was a class structure to the American car, as there was to the cars built in other countries. But in the fifties the class lines blurred as low-priced cars took on the glamour, the power and the performance of prestige cars. A 1955 Chevrolet Bel Air had far less social status than a 1955 Cadillac de Ville, but it had the same basic contours and styling, and, for the first time, equal performance. Before the overhead-valve V8 became the standard American car engine, highway power and performance were measures of prestige that distinguished expensive cars from economy cars. Luxury cars traditionally had bigger engines with more cylinders and more horsepower. The overhead-valve V8 in the mid-fifties changed all that, giving lighter economy cars an advantage.

The love of power and speed seems to be a natural human appetite. Men raced horses before they raced cars, and raced on foot before that. But no other national population has grown up with so much opportunity to indulge the love of speed on wheels. Ever since Ford began mass production in 1912, there have been cars in used-car lots, cars in junkyards and cast-off engines for sale in garages for people to tinker with and experiment to improvise their own vehicles. The American tradition of hot-rodding and customizing goes back to the early years of the century. It gained national attention as a Californian cultural phenomenon in the early fifties when most American boys in the fifties wanted a hot-rod and American girls wanted a convertible. Both were different interpretations of glamour on wheels. By the end of the fifties, Detroit was building Chevys, Fords and Plymouths with all the power and speed hot-rodders dreamed of, with

convertibles in every model line and range.

Songs, movies and books of every decade feature cars as prominently as they do hairstyles, clothes and slang. Hot-rods, custom cars, cruising, drag racing and cars for surfing became part of American pop culture. They were prominent in movies, in pop records, on TV and radio. The generation that grew up after World War II enjoyed a sense of personal power through the automobile unlike that experienced by citizens of any other culture or country. By the end of the fifties, the easy availability of big, powerful, glamorous cars was accepted without question, almost as an American birthright. It coloured American thinking about the nation's role in the world, as a country with limitless resources, power and privilege. The shiny, powerful V8 cars were the promise of tomorrow available today. Cars were a visible symbol of success for every American to enjoy, new or second-hand.

Cars in Europe, where gas was expensive and disposable income scarce, did more with less, encouraging the technology of efficiency. American car-makers did more with more and refused to change the shape or context of cars that continued to sell. Performance and glamorous styling continued to lead the wish-list for most American car-buyers of the sixties, though change was clearly coming. Detroit answered the appeal of the Volkswagen and other small imports with three domestic imitations: the Corvair, the Falcon and the Valiant. A decade later the Corvair was gone, the Falcon and Valiant had outgrown their mission, and another generation of compacts took their places.

Dream cars continued to matter, and the dream continued to be power and glamour. But the American interpretation of the dream on wheels crashed in the economic and ecological crises of the seventies and Detroit's efforts to imitate imports failed. A decade of chequered attempts at new automotive directions in domestic cars changed the balance of the American auto market. Imports went from a fraction to a chunk that represented a quarter of the market in the early eighties.

By 1980, American taste in cars had been indelibly altered by the influence of foreign cars. The dream was no longer all-American. German, Italian and Japanese cars carried as much prestige, performance and glamour as American cars. The American performance car temporarily lost its power to emission and mileage regulations and German, Japanese and Italian cars led the way. Porsche, Mercedes-Benz, Ferrari and BMW replaced American models as top status cars, and hot-rodding became the pastime of the rich determined to have the fastest and the best Porsche. Customized Porsches, Ferraris, BMWs and Mercedes-Benzs were the new status cars of the newly rich and became part of the new American dream.

But in the second half of the eighties, American cars came back with more of the thrilling V8 performance that was supposed to have passed into history. The Mustang, the Corvette and the Camaro were world-class performance cars again, with gas prices at an all-time low and technology at an all-time high. The American dream car was still on the road.

THE EARLY FIFTIES

Post-war prosperity, the overhead-valve V8 and the new look of luxury on wheels for everyone

A construction and employment boom after World War II put more people to work at better wages than at any other time in history. Wartime research development of aircraft engine technology produced the automative advance of the decade: the overhead-valve, high-compression V8. Cadillac and Oldsmobile featured OHV V8 power that led performance standards for the time. Harley Earl's low, wide and handsome American look shaped the design of the decade, and the low-priced economy Ford and Chevrolet took on the glamorous look of luxury cars.

THE American horsepower race was already under way in 1950 when Cadillac emerged from the cocoon of dreary post-war styling with a flamboyant new definition of automotive glamour for the fifties. With 160hp from an advanced new high-compression V8 engine, Cadillac immediately became the performance king of the American road.

The new motor had been launched by General Motors engineers Harry and Ed Cole in the 1949 Oldsmobiles and Cadillacs. Wartime research development for military aircraft had taken the internal-combustion gasoline piston engine to the outer limits of performance, before the jet turbine retired the propeller-plane in 1945. By exploiting the results of this pioneering aircraft engine development, GM researchers were able to usher in a new high-technology age for the automobile engine. With valves in the cylinder heads instead of the cylinder-block walls as in most car engines of the time, the new motor could breathe better, and it produced more power from enhanced combustion of gases compressed to higher density. In fact, the 160hp output of the 1949 Cadillac V8 barely tapped the potential of the 331 cubic-inch engine. But it was enough to make Cadillac the fastest American sedan.

It is unlikely that many Cadillac buyers knew or cared about the new technology under the hood, however, because high performance was expected in a luxury car. Superior power and highway performance had been prerequisites of the luxury marques from the beginning. Pierce Arrow, Packard, Lincoln, Duesenberg, Cadillac and other prestige cars all offered bigger engines with more cylinders, more power and more speed than low-priced cars. During the flapper years of the Jazz Age in the twenties, luxury cars boasted massive V8s, V12s and V16s, while the Ford Model T and Model A made do with only four cylinders. Expense of production subsequently phased out the V16s and most of the V12s, so that eight cylinders had become the norm for American luxury cars before World War II. The fifties were to witness an escalating power race through intensive development of the overhead-valve V8s, which would take over as the standard American passenger car engine by 1955.

The selling feature of the 1950 Cadillac was not horsepower, though. It was styling. While Lincoln,

Right: 1949 Cadillac Coupe de Ville
Head GM stylist Harley Earl said the new Cadillac design was inspired by the twin-tail P-38 World War II fighter plane. The flamboyant Earl described the extravagant new design as 'graceful bulk'.

Below: 1951 Mercury Convertible
1950s America was seeing a dream come real, and the wide, low, streamlined Mercury was the shape of the good life on wheels. The rounded contours and soft edges made Mercury a favourite of Californian customizers and hot-rodders, and gave America power at a price most people could afford.

Streaking over the open road the **1951 MERCURY** *gives you real excitement*

Chrysler and Packard still had late-forties shapes, Cadillac took on an all-new look of lush flamboyance that was to be the style of the fifties. American luxury cars of the thirties had reflected the traditions of elegant European and English coachbuilding. In the forties the high-sided, low-window shapes created a cloistered image intended to evoke express trains and ocean liners. By 1950, this was a dated look rendered musty and dull by the new shape of Cadillac.

Wide and low with sweeping sheet-metal planes and sensuous curves, the 1950 Cadillac had upswept rear fenders ending in tailfins which GM head stylist Harley Earl said were inspired by the twin-tail P-38 World War II fighter-plane. Earl's words and concepts were as flamboyant as the designs he presided over: he called the new Cadillac styling 'graceful bulk', and coined the term 'dynamic obsolescence' for the Detroit practice of producing new sheet metal each year to make the previous year's cars look out of date, so that owners would trade them in for new models.

'Graceful bulk' was apt for the new Cadillac. It could also have been called an elegant hunk, with compound curves, slabs of chrome and overstatement in every line. There was nothing subtle about it. The grille was an imposing chrome esplanade with a pair of chrome grille-sprits called 'Dagmars', after a busty TV actress popular at the time. The tailfins generated a great many jokes about styling indulgence and design excess. They also started the dominant trend in US passenger car styling for the fifties and much of the sixties.

The Series 62 Cadillac convertible was so handsome it could practically stop traffic with its looks alone. It removed any lingering doubt that the grey years of wartime austerity and the immediate post-war period, with their shortages, ration stops and limited supplies, were finally over. The new Cadillac was a fifties American dream on wheels, a lush statement of power, luxury and the glamour of success.

Cadillac advertising stressed elegance and taste, but the real pride of Cadillac ownership was being wealthy enough to buy one. A 1950 Cadillac convertible cost $3650 when the average house sold for $10 000 and the average yearly wage was $3000. The official American dream of the twentieth century was that every native-born American could be President, but the average American heart and mind were more set

Left: 1949 Cadillac Coupe de Ville
The Cadillac convertible was so handsome it removed all doubt that the grey war years were over. Cadillac's modern look in the fifties broke a styling chain dating back to the time luxury cars were designed to accommodate men wearing top hats. The Coupe de Ville and convertible Coupe had sharply raked roof lines that were too low for men wearing hats. With red leather upholstery, silver 'sombrero' wheel covers and chrome accents everywhere, Cadillac was designed to dazzle.

Right: 1951 Ford Crestliner
The triple-name 'Custom Deluxe Crestliner' made clear the direction American car-makers were going: to decorate and then decorate on top of the decorations to make cars as irresistable as ice-cream sundaes. The Crestliner boasted a bold two-tone styling treatment with a scalloped side panel in a contrasting colour and shaped like a cross-section of an aeroplane wing. It was the third year of the slab-sided, bullet-styled Ford with a double-spinner grille to differentiate it from the 1950 model.

on owning a home with a new car in the garage than moving to the White House. And in 1950, more Americans were able to buy homes and cars than ever before. Jobs were plentiful in a post-war economic boom that had not yet been slowed by inflation. Houses were easy to purchase with low-interest Veteran Administration loans that also put World War II vets through college. Stores were loaded with new consumer goods available on the instalment plan, so every new house could have a new TV, a new refrigerator and a new washing machine. Most Americans were not affluent. Most had not reached middle-class status. But the level of material comfort, and purchasing power on the never-never, was higher for most Americans than ever before. Cars, which had been scarce and expensive during the wartime production halt, were bigger and better than ever.

Cadillac was the biggest and best of all. The 1950 Cadillac was 17 ft 10 in long and weighed 3900 pounds – just short of 2 tons. At $3200, that works out to $178 a foot and $0.82 a pound, compared to Ford and Chevrolet which sold for $0.50 a pound and $91 a

1953 Cadillac Eldorado
The fifties were a new age of convenience and leisure. The strong, square-hipped, broad-shouldered contours of the Cadillac with shaved-down tailfins, was the luxury look America wanted.

foot. Chrysler, Packard and Lincoln cost just as much for each foot and each pound weight as Cadillac did, but Cadillac was ahead in style and power. Chrysler would offer an overhead-valve, high-compression V8 the following year and Lincoln would do the same in 1952, but Cadillac led the luxury-car pack at the start of the decade.

Harley Earl probably knew better than anyone else that styling, not engineering, sold American cars. The modern, aggressive look he gave Cadillac in 1950 broke a styling chain dating back to the thirties and before, when luxury cars were designed to accommodate men wearing top hats. The 1950 Cadillac Series 62 Coup de Ville and convertible coupe had a sharply raked roof that was too low for men wearing hats. With red leather upholstery, silver 'sombrero' wheel covers and chrome accents everywhere, a 1950 Cadillac de Ville was designed to dazzle, and it succeeded. But it was more than a handsome shape. The 1950 Cadillac Series 62 offered the luxury of an automatic transmission to relieve privileged Americans of the burden of shifting their own gears.

While early-fifties America had the dark fear of the Russians and the hydrogen bomb, the Rosenberg executions and the McCarthy hearings, it was also the time of Eisenhower and of glamour marriages – Eddie Fisher and Elizabeth Taylor, Marilyn Monroe and Joe DiMaggio. The fifties were Roy Rogers, the Lone Ranger, Guy Lombardo, Perry Como, the Honeymooners, Ozzie & Harriet, the Hula Hoop, the dishwasher, the pre-fab house, the pop-up toaster, colour TV, home power tools and portable radios. American images of success and privilege came from TV, movies, and advertisements in magazines and on billboards. The image of Cadillac ownership was a gleaming car at the entrance of a country club; a convertible cruising the Strip in Las Vegas at night with the wail of a saxophone in the background; a Cadillac in front of a lush hotel bordered by royal palms on Miami Beach. It was an image few Americans ever saw realized, but millions imagined. And it was part of their dream that the pop culture heroes of TV and movies drove Cadillacs in those very places. Some of them did.

In 1950, sales of 110 000 cars took the total number of Cadillacs sold since 1908 past the one million mark. The fifties were a new age of convenience. America had a growing appetite for leisure and luxury, and Cadillac was the look of luxury on wheels most Americans wanted. The style that had been so bold and new for 1950 established itself as the standard look for the

American luxury car, only getting lower and longer-looking in the succeeding years. Other styling approaches were tried and found wanting by a public that rejected everything outside the mainstream. By 1955, the strong, square-hipped, broad-shouldered outline of the Cadillac with shaved-down tailfins, was *the* look of the American car.

Cadillac advertised horsepower without mentioning performance. Before the introduction of the new V8 in 1949, Oldsmobile ads omitted power, focusing on the virtues of quality, reliability and smart styling. A forties Olds ad described the car as 'Styled to Lead, and Built to Last'. But in 1950 Oldsmobile advertising emphasized the power and performance of the new Rocket V8 and called the new shape 'Futuramic'.

The new Oldsmobile shape for the fifties was essentially Cadillac without tailfins. Instead of the twin-bullet grille, Oldsmobile had twin-cylindrical decorative abutments protruding from the mouth of a grille as massive as Cadillac's. The 1951 Olds 98 introduced the horizontal rear fender line which would become the dominant auto silhouette of the decade. Given the auto ad-makers' taste for clichés in promoting styling concepts, or attempting to conceal the lack of them, the new Olds rear fender line might have been labelled 'backswept, direct-flow rear fender'. Or 'DynaFlow' fenders, if Buick had not taken that name for their new automatic transmission.

The new rear fenders gave the Olds 98 a jet-age look appropriate to the ads showing cars positioned in front of jets and rockets, with happy young couples riding the Rocket hood ornament. The oblong, rectangular fender broke a tradition of rear fenders contoured over the radius of the rear wheel, which in the thirties had taken a semi-teardrop shape known as the French Curve that would later be called streamlined. The new flush fender line of the Oldsmobile did not reflect the wheel radius at all. Instead, the fender extended in a flat, horizontal plane beyond the end of the trunk lid, squaring off the tail of the car in profile. It made the 98 appear longer, and the angularity made it look unmistakably modern.

In 1951, the new look of the top-line 98 was extended to the lower-priced 88 series and a new model was created featuring the 98 motor in a dressed-up 88 for a bargain-performer called the Super 88.

Left and above:
1951 Oldsmobile Rocket 88
Essentially Cadillac without tailfins, the new Oldsmobile shape for the fifties was called 'Futuramic'. With twin-cylindrical decorative abutments instead of Cadillac's twin-bullet grille, Oldsmobile introduced the horizontal rear fender line which would become the dominant auto silhouette of the decade.

Right: **1952 Buick 'Dynaflow'**
The name 'Dynaflow' for the Buick automatic transmission blended the two elements of fifties' car merchandising: the dynamic power and effortless flow of automatic gears.

BUICK *with Dynaflow Drive for 1952*

With Cadillac performance at little over half the Cadillac price, the Super 88 was an immediate success. At $2200, the moderate-priced glamour image attracted a younger, more adventurous buyer than Cadillac. The new Oldsmobile image was romance, excitement, good looks, speed and power, which seemed to be what a great many people wanted in a car. The Olds 98 and the Super 88 offered much more than the virtuous reliability, sound engineering and sensible styling marketed in the forties. The new Oldsmobile was more than a means of transport. It was a car for driving pleasure, built to satisfy that desire for travel for its own sake that seems to be a basic trait of the American character.

Important chapters of American history were written by the movement of people in social and economic migrations that shaped and resettled the country. John Steinbeck chronicled the desperate years of the Great Depression, for instance, when masses of Mid-Westerners drove west for a better life. But in the second half of the twentieth century, mobility on wheels was more an expression of social freedom and recreation, of travel for the sake of movement, than a desire or need to get somewhere. Driving, going somewhere, going nowhere, was becoming a pastime. Just cruising: cruising at night to the music of a radio with the drone of a powerful motor in the background.

Cruising was a pursuit of freedom in a leisure society, and the pleasure people took in it related to the image of the car they drove. The Olds Super 88 had the looks, it had the style, it had the V8 to turn a wish into motion with mere pressure on the gas pedal. The Olds Rocket 88 was a cruiser with a motor big enough to make anyone powerful. Oldsmobile was not a cheap car, but it was not as far out of reach for the non-wealthy as a Cadillac. An Olds 88 was a car to dream about owning in the belief that the dream might come true.

Harley Earl had a simple explanation for the success of the new look of Cadillac and Oldsmobile. He said a rectangle or oblong shape was nicer to look at than a square box. In 1950, Lincoln had a flowing, aerodynamic look that hardly had a straight line in it. For the 1952 model year, Lincoln went rectangular with an angular shape featuring horizontal, knife-edge fender lines with planes and angles instead of curves. It was a clean, new look, sharp and crisp without rounded contours or accents. It was a look Lincoln would follow through the sixties, and in 1952 it was still unspoiled by excess chrome trim or styling gimmickry.

Lincoln introduced a new 160hp overhead-valve V8 with the new styling, but Cadillac was already leading the undeclared horsepower race with 190hp in 1952. For 1953, Cadillac advertised power was up to 210hp and Lincoln raised its to 205. That was the year Lincoln made its legend as a hot-rod luxury car by sweeping its class first, second, third and fourth in the punishing, dangerous Pan American Road Race across Mexico. Another team of factory-entered Lincolns won again in Mexico the following year. There was no factory Cadillac entry in the Mexican road race because the

Cadillac image implied performance superiority without having to stoop to prove it. The Ford Motor Company was out to prove that Lincoln was faster and pursued a full Lincoln racing programme which included the stock car circuit, where Lincoln was a formidable challenger to Hudson and Oldsmobile.

The sharp, contemporary styling and abundant power made the 1951 and 1953 Lincolns strong successes on the market and the performance mystique of the powerful Lincoln engine inspired a 1960 hit record called *Hot-Rod Lincoln*. The song was the rockabilly guitar boogie story of a street race between a Cadillac and a Lincoln-powered Ford hot-rod.

1952 Lincoln Capri
Romances about fast American cars have been written about cars with V8 engines. One of the most potent was the 205hp Lincoln, which swept the Pan American Road Race two years in a row. Its performance mystique inspired the 1960 hit record 'Hot Rod Lincoln'.

Recorded by Johnny Bond and written by Ryan Stevenson, it had a theme that was central to backyard hot-rodding: the conquest of a Cadillac by a home-built car.

Most of the romances about fast American cars have been written about cars with V8 engines. Though there have been six-cylinder cars that outran eight-cylinder cars, the six has not generated the songs and stories inspired by the V8. But one six that deserved and got its own chapter in the book of American social history of the fifties is the mighty Hudson Hornet.

The Hornet appeared in 1951, a high-performance version of a radically unorthodox body style introduced in 1948. Though American auto design evolved into a common style by 1956, body shapes were still dramatically varied in 1950. Studebaker, Nash and Hudson produced cars that resembled fighter-plane fuselages or wing-tanks more than the GM shape which prevailed for the fifties. The 1949–51 Studebaker looked something like a light aircraft without wings; the 1949 Nash was said to resemble a bath tub. The 1949 Hudson looked like nothing else on the road. If it

races in the National Association for Stock Car Auto Racing (NASCAR) series, including the Southern 500 at Darlington, South Carolina, in 1951. In 1952, the Hudson Hornet team won 27 out of 34 Grand National races on the NASCAR circuit, racking up a total of 40 wins in 48 major stock-car races.

Stock-car racing was more popular in the South than in the rest of the country, but the racetrack wins fuelled the Hudson legend which was woven into narrative in the pages of Jack Kerouac's *On the Road*. Kerouac's 1957 novel was a lyrical celebration of driving in search of fulfilment or kicks, whichever came first. The book contained breathless, jagged accounts of frantic dashes across the country in a 1949 Hudson, bought on sight from a San Francisco used-car lot on instalments that were never paid, after the first one. The hedonistic trips in *On the Road* resonated with the dark currents of modern jazz that was the gospel of the sub-culture of the hipsters in Kerouac's books, men who travelled at night following the white line down an unexplored back road to the sound of jazz on the car radio.

The Hudson in Kerouac's book was an escape vehicle from what he and other writers, labelled as spokesmen of the Beat Generation, saw as the horrors of suburban conformity that was spreading over America like a cultural lava flow. But the rootless, high-speed wandering could just as well have been a metaphor for the American urge to explore, move and travel which had been central to American literature from Walt Whitman's time onwards. Mark Twain and John Steinbeck wrote of westward movement for both adventure and hope of a better life. The car travel in Kerouac's books always had a destination, but the trips usually ended up being travel for its own sake, with a spirit of romantic wandering that was part of the myth of the American cowboys, and the explorers before them. After World War II, this craving to be on the move was expressed mainly in driving the nation's highways.

The 1949 Hudson that caught the eye of the hipster protagonist of *On the Road* featured new technology derived from aircraft construction in which body and chassis were built as a unit instead of separately. That put Hudson ahead of other Detroit auto-makers, at least in theory. Unit construction allowed for a dropped floorpan which put the floorboards below the door-sills. This in turn made for a low centre of gravity and led to the cars being nicknamed 'step-downs'. The low centre of gravity gave Hudson excellent

suggested anything, it might have been a restyled, aerodynamic PT boat. Slab-sided, slope-backed in a smooth rearward flow that looked both streamlined and massive with great girth and bulk, the Hudson looked powerful and fast. It was.

With an enormous 300-inch six (actually 308 cubic-inch) that was much larger than the Ford, Chevrolet and Oldsmobile V8s, the Hudson Hornet was a monster motor. It put out 145hp with an aluminium high-compression 'power-dome' cylinder head as standard equipment. The street Hudson Hornets were identified by a special 'Badge of Power' – a rocketship with Hornet lettering on the side mouldings and on the trunk. The 145hp Hornet was able to compete on equal terms with a Cadillac or Oldsmobile in a highway speed contest, but the Hudson legend grew most swiftly out of the factory-modified cars that raced on the sands of Daytona Beach and stock-car tracks throughout the South.

The factory racing Hudsons were equipped with special performance engine options listed under the category of 'severe usage', including a 'Twin H-power' option with dual carburettors and a 7-X racing engine package which boosted horsepower to 210 in 1953. A modified Hudson Hornet was timed at 112 mph and the factory-backed cars won 12 Grand National

1953 Hudson Hornet
The Hudson Hornets were identified by a special 'Badge of Power' that announced the potent 145hp aluminium-head, high-compression engine. The Hornet was able to compete on equal terms with Cadillac or Oldsmobile on the highway, and Hudson became a car of legend through wins by factory-modified cars at Daytona Beach and southern stock-car tracks.

manoeuvrability on the racetrack, which was part of the reason Hudson dominated stock-car racing until 1954. The other qualities were the high power output of the Twin H-power and 7-X engine, and the factory commitment to competition.

But the racetrack wins never translated into street sales success, possibly because of the Hudson's unusual styling. Americans were ready for a new look for the fifties, but not the Hudson look. People wanted, it turned out, something just like what everybody else had, and the Hudson was different. The Hudson was also expensive – $1000 more than an Olds 88 and only slightly less than a Cadillac Series 61. Too much to pay

1954 Studebaker Commander
The 1953–4 Studebaker was a stunning styling effort that failed. As sleek and elegant of line as any European sports car of the time, the 1953–4 Studebaker celebrated the company's 100th anniversary, and was well received by everyone except the people who counted: the public.

for a radically different-looking car with an old-fashioned motor that developed power through sheer size and brute strength rather than modern technology. Before the fifties were over, Hudson and the giant L-head six would be history, but not forgotten.

Another distinctive styling effort that failed in the market-place was the stunning 1953 Studebaker, attributed to Raymond Loewy. A daring, innovative two-door coupe that was as sleek and elegant of line as any European sports car of the time, the 1953 model was intended as a celebration of Studebaker's 100th anniversary in the travel vehicle business. The Studebaker was very well received by critics and highly praised for its design by everyone but the people who counted – the American public. Studebaker was in shaky financial health at the time, and the brilliant, original styling of the 1953 hardtop coupe was out of the mainstream of American taste. That meant the car was doomed.

Cadillacs and Lincolns were the cars people saw as symbols of success in movies, on TV and in magazine advertisements, but Chevrolets, Fords and Plymouths were the cars most people drove. Eighteen people bought Chevrolets for every Cadillac purchased in 1950, and there were 20 Fords sold for every Lincoln in 1952. So the real contest between manufacturers was the battle for sales of the low-priced three. The competition got white hot in the fifties. The seller's market that followed the war, with new car supply short of buyer demand, had now turned into a buyer's market. Production had finally caught up with demand; the great rush to own a new car had been satisfied. Dealers had to work for every sale and auto-makers tried to turn every model-change into an exciting major event.

Chevrolet and Ford were brand-new cars for the 1949–50 model years. With the new Bel Air line,

Chevrolet had evolved from plain economy family car to stylish modern, with a two-door hardtop coupe and convertible coupe model that was unmistakably glamorous. Glamour was something new for Chevrolet. It was new for any economy car. The selling points of Detroit's lower-cost cars had been practicality, reliability and economy. But that was not enough for the marketing decision-makers of the fifties, who believed customers wanted as much sparkle and glitter for their dollar as they could get. The 1950 Chevrolet Bel Air hardtop coupe was a design without window-posts, with a cut-cornered roof and wrap-around rear glass that gave the car an elegance previously featured only in more expensive cars.

With the Blue Flame six-cylinder motor, the Chevrolet was not an exciting performer, but the average car buyer apparently cared less about speed than the new Chevrolet image. GM's low-priced volume leader was chic and smart in 1950, a car with the look of success. And Chevrolet offered the indulgence of shiftless driving with the new Powerglide automatic transmission. Like Cadillac's 'Hydramatic' automatic transmission and Buick's 'DynaFlow', the

1951 Ford Convertible
The convertible with its top down suggested the romance of the carefree, adventurous life that could be enjoyed by anyone bold enough to buy a convertible.

Overleaf: **1950 Chevrolet Styleline De Luxe**
The 1950s saw Chevrolet make a dramatic transition. From a conservative style that suggested the virtues of thrift, practicality and reliability, the low-priced GM car metamorphosed into something graceful and elegant. With the model name Bel Air came svelte, continental glamour. The Chevrolet convertible presented the image of carefree, romantic adventure that had previously been the province of luxury cars. The power of luxury-car performance would come a few years later with the V8.

27

Powerglide name suggested both power and convenience – a perfect metaphor for the American automotive taste. Chevrolet sales hit 1.5 million cars in 1950, the second model year of the new smooth, flowing shape it shared with Oldsmobile and Pontiac. It was an all-time sales record for Chevrolet.

Ford tried a different shape for glamour in 1950 with a sleek, slab-sided bullet profile. This was replaced in 1952 by a sharp, angular design with the lines of the Lincoln of the same year. Chevrolet styling was ahead of Ford in 1950, but Ford took the lead back with its 1952 styling and pulled further in front with a new overhead-valve V8 in 1954.

Performance had always been part of Ford's image, with the flathead V8 that dated directly back to 1932. It was the economy car with power, the working man's V8. Largely because of the V8 motor, Ford was the make chosen by most American police departments in the early fifties, adding to the Ford image of power and speed. While the roving cowboy of the Wild West was still a staple of American film and TV entertainment during the fifties, the Lone Ranger and Roy Rogers were giving way to contemporary police detective TV shows, and millions of Americans watched actor Broderick Crawford drive California highways in a 1950 Ford in *Highway Patrol*. That show was later

1950 Mercury Sedan
Ford's look for the early 1950s, seen in Mercury as well, was a slab-sided, bullet-profiled car. With the V8 that had been Ford's power advantage since 1932, Mercurys and Fords were the performance leaders for the average American. The Ford V8 was the working man's fast car, and the car most often used for police work. The American cowboy spirit of the Wild West gave way to the roving police patrol in 1950s' television, with Broderick Crawford ranging the California highways in *Highway Patrol* in a 1950 Ford.

eclipsed by *Dragnet* and the unsmiling face of Jack Webb as a Los Angeles police detective, but Ford was still there – Webb cruised the streets in a 1953 model. Ford's days as the popular-priced performance car would end with the Chevrolet V8 (1955), but in 1953 Ford was unchallenged by Chevrolet as the car to beat, and third-place Plymouth had not yet developed either the power or glamour to pose serious competition.

For every one of the millions of Americans who could afford to buy new cars in the early fifties, there were many millions more who could not. For them, the choice was used cars, the second- or third-hand dream cars. Used cars were usually the only cars within reach of teenagers, who seemed to be the ones most concerned with glamour and performance and the ones least able to pay for it. They were a new after-school leisure class with luxury-car taste and second-hand economy-car spending money.

In the prosperity that followed World War II, American teenagers had remarkable freedom for their age group, and played a major part in the extraordinarily high automobile ownership rate of post-war America, an average that rose from one car per family in the early fifties to two cars per family by the end of the decade. Cars were primarily recreation vehicles, not transport, for teenagers. With cars they could escape the world of school rules, of home and grown-ups in general, to enjoy a world guided by rules of their own. If cars were symbols of status and success to American adults, they were symbols of identity to teenagers. Car clubs with club jackets sprang up at high schools across the country and car ownership became one of the most desired things in life. Still, few fifties teenagers could afford their own cars, and most of them drove their parents' instead. But those with jobs or generous allowances bought cars from used-car

For teenagers in the fifties, rock 'n' roll music and fast cars were symbols of revolt, and both were features of the classic 1955 film *Rebel Without a Cause*. In that movie, and others, American teenagers wandered in search of freedom and fulfillment in cars that grown-ups called hot-rods, which were most likely based on Fords.

lots, which in the mid-fifties were rich territory for bargain auto shoppers. In 1954, a 1946 or 1947 Ford or Chevrolet cost between $50 and $100 on monthly instalments at a used-car lot. An older car could be picked up for even less.

The older cars were the ones made into hot-rods for the speed and glamour which post-war American teenagers seemed to see as their birthright. The favoured make for hot-rod cars was Ford, and there were favoured years also: 1940 and 1941 two-door sedans, coupes and roadsters, and two-door coupes

and roadsters from any of the thirties model years. The thirties Fords, with their racy, stylish lines, light weight and V8 power, were natural starting-point vehicles for hot-rodders out to build a dream car.

Building a dream car was the answer for the millions who could not afford a new car but had to have something powerful and distinctive. Home-built specials, hot-rods and custom cars were common enough to be an indigenous automotive sub-species in southern California. Hot-rodding flourished there as early as the twenties and spread after the war. In the beginning, hot-rodding was simple tinkering with an engine to squeeze out more power for better performance.

Then it was transplanting a junkyard Model A motor into a Model T to make it go faster than Henry Ford intended. When the V8 Ford was introduced in 1932, it immediately became the motor hot-rodders stuffed in older, lighter cars.

The mechanics and metal-workers drawn to the Los Angeles area by the aircraft production based there in World War II provided a resource pool for hot-rodders. They produced special engine parts which hot-rodders used to rebuild their V8s to make more power. A hot-rod Model A Ford with a modified V8, or a cut-down Model T hot-rod with a V8 could out-accelerate and outrun an expensive new car.

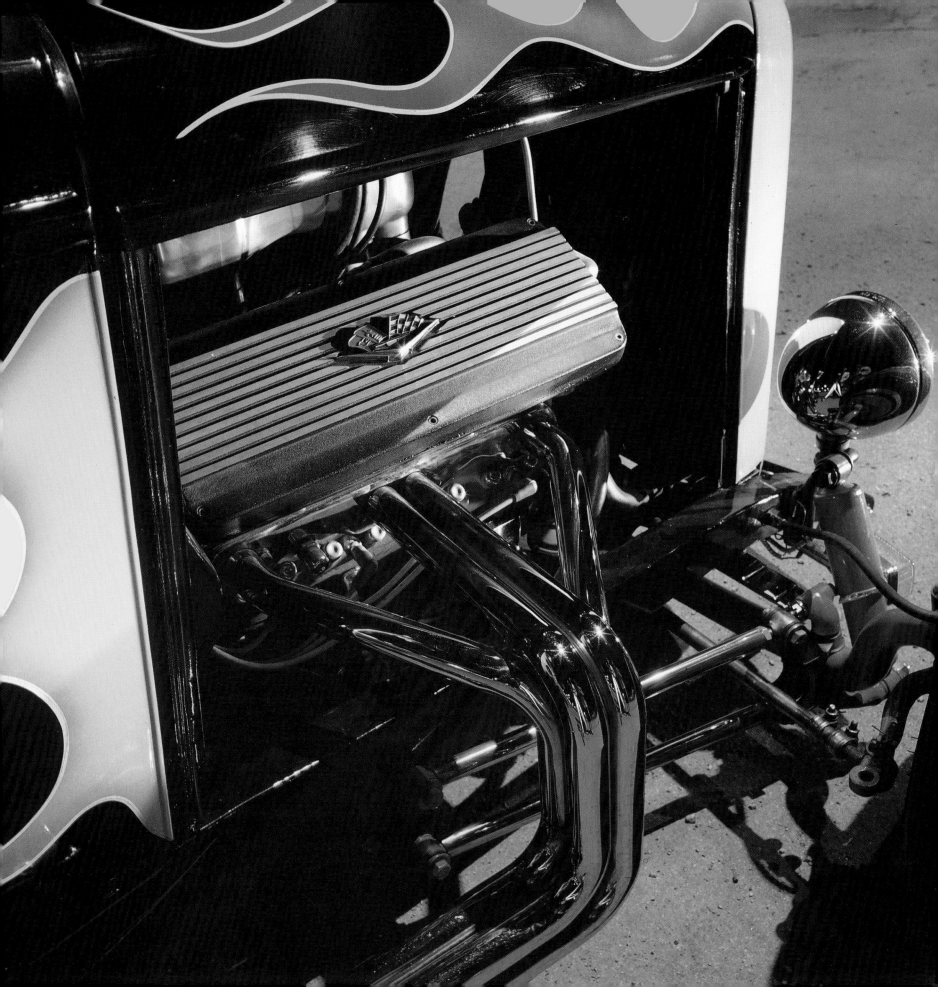

1951 Mercury 'Low-rider'
Hot-rods had souped-up engines in older cars, with bodies cut down and lightened for speed. They had trim and paint custom-tailored for style, which was just as important as speed. The favoured cars for hot-rodding and customizing were Fords, for the looks and V8 motors, and Mercurys, for the same reasons. The droopy, melted look of the 1950 and 1951 Mercury was a natural for customizing. It almost looked customized to begin with.

Left: **1937 Ford Hot-rod**
The flat-faced grille of the early thirties Fords gave way to a streamline, modern look shown by this 1937 model. Fifty years later, the 1937 Ford remains a favourite of hot-rodders and customizers.

Below: in the early 1950s drag racing tracks had opened for sanctioned contests, but the outlaw form of racing on the street lived on. This scene from the popular 1973 movie *American Graffiti* shows the classic face-off confrontation of the old and the new: a 1932 Ford hot-rod against a 1955 Chevrolet.

Hot-rodding was do-it-yourself mechanics, an expression of the American's urge to change, the compulsion to alter and improve the car he owned to outperform the car he could not afford. The goal of hot-rodding, besides enjoying the performance produced by the hot-rodder's own ingenuity, was to build cars that could beat the cars the rich guys drove.

The initiates-only nature of hot-rodding appealed to the teenager's desire for a separate, private world. Hot-rods and custom cars were unique, special vehicles that identified their owners as special and unique too. Hot-rodders turned vintage Fords – and Mercurys, which later became just as popular – into high-powered machines with souped-up engines and restyling which ranged from subtle to flamboyant. The serious hot-rodding was done by people who were skilled with wrenches and comfortable dismantling and reassembling engines, or auto-body men who were experts at sheet-metal work. For the average teen-ager with a second-hand car and a desire to be different, there was the simple adding of fender skirts, dual exhaust-pipe extensions, outside spotlights, front windshield visors and special paint.

The custom look that evolved in California in the late forties emerged as a thread of American pop culture in the fifties. The California look was a clean look, a

reaction against overstatement and exaggerated chrome trim on new cars in the second half of the fifties. California car customizers removed exterior chrome trim, sanded the body flush and covered it with dozens of coats of lacquer. Chrome was saved for the engine compartment, the one area Detroit stylists ignored; hot-rodders chromed every engine part that could be chromed. Bodies were lowered on frames, interiors were custom-upholstered, roofs were chopped and lowered. Door handles were removed and replaced by inside latches for a smoother look.

The cars which were built for speed had extensively modified engines, usually lifted from a much later

Right: **1951 Mercury 'Low-rider'**
The 1951 Mercury achieved automotive immortality as the car James Dean drove in *Rebel Without a Cause*, but even before the movie was made the Mercury's bulbous, low-down lines had made it a strong favourite with car customizers.

1934 Ford Hot-rod Coupe

The classic 1930s' Ford came in many variations and model years. Styling changed continuously from 1930 onward, with each year bringing a new flair to an already stylish look. The 1932, 1933 and 1934 Fords were all popular with hot-rodders for the same reasons: they were sleek, light and glamorous from the start. Customized with the underground artisan's touch, they acquired an elegance of design and statement equal to anything on the road.

Overleaf: **1932 Ford 'Deuce Coupe'**

The 1932 Ford coupe had the most favoured shape of all the cars used for hot-rodding. In the fifties it picked up the name 'Deuce Coupe' and a stylishly customized rod like this one was the highest status symbol an American teenager dreamed of in the early 1950s. The stark angles of the basic design contrast with the flow of the curves in the hood, fenders and rear deck to give an elegance of line that loses nothing with time.

model car. The most radical hot-rods were 1932 Ford two-door roadsters and coupes with overhead-valve V8s from Cadillacs or Oldsmobiles. Cad- and Olds-powered rods were the hottest things on wheels in the early fifties, and were all but unbeatable in drag racing and the illegal street racing it evolved from.

No one knows exactly how or when drag racing developed as a native American sport, but it probably grew out of the desire to see just what a car could do. That meant trying it out against another car pulling away from a stoplight or stop sign. Informal stoplight-to-speed contests led to sanctioned one-against-one, straight-line races called drag racing in the late forties. Because a drag race could happen almost anywhere two drivers lined up, it was a recreational pastime that rivalled baseball in popularity. In the early fifties, drag racing strips were opened throughout southern California and across the country, and drag racing was on the way to becoming a national sport and a major industry.

Although older Fords were the cheapest buys for hot-rodding, and their sleek, rakish lines made the most classic rods, late model cars were also popular with the average teenager, who liked to drive the closest thing to a new car he could afford. The 1949-51 Mercury had the look of a custom hot-rod almost as it came from the factory. With a sleek, windswept, melting-curve shape that appealed to hot-rodders and teenagers when it was new, the 1949-51 Merc two-door sedan was popular well into the sixties. The 1951 Merc achieved a cult car status with a movie role as James Dean's car in *Rebel Without a Cause*, the 1955 Hollywood portrayal of the rebellious, mis-understood American teenager in an unsympathetic grown-up society. The movie made a legend of Dean, who died in a car accident the year it was released, and the car became an instant classic. It had the high-styled lines of a car already customized, but the customized Mercs popular in California before and after *Rebel* took the styling beyond the factory treatment into a low, sinister dream car that was at once threatening and seductive.

A full-blown custom car built by George Barris or one of the other major names in California custom-car making was a major body-building production, but the biggest effort in most custom rods was engine work. Moving parts were replaced by custom parts specially built for light weight and high performance. All visible engine components were shined and polished if they could not be chromed. Hot-rod engines were designed

1932 Ford 'Deuce Coupe'

In the second half of the fifties 1932 Ford roadsters and coupes underwent engine transplants to be powered by souped-up Chevrolet V8s like this one. But the classic shape of the Ford prevailed as a statement of style, even four decades later when most of the designs of its era had passed into obscurity.

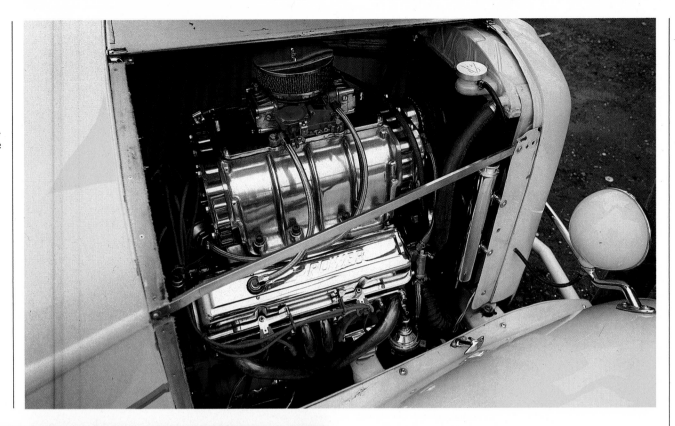

to dazzle when the hood was opened. Instead of a greasy, grey-black motor and wiring, there was a gleaming, shiny display of polished chrome and sparkling, spotless metal.

The real purpose of hot-rodding was speed, and at speed hot-rods were supreme. A fully built 1932 Ford roadster with a full-race V8 flathead or a transplanted Olds or Cad V8 had more horsepower than a new Olds or a Cadillac, and less than two-thirds the weight. That enabled hot-rods to humiliate brand-new luxury cars in street races, and in the early fifties the California hot-rodder in Levis and tee-shirt with a cigarette in his sleeve could call his hot-rod the performance king of the road.

But style was almost as important as speed to hot-rodders, especially in California where 'looking good' was as important as going fast. With the absolute dictates of the clique, high style in hot-rods became an aesthetic imperative. A rod had to look good or subject its owner to discrimination by his peers. The properly prepared hot-rod – a 1932 Ford roadster or five-window coupe – was low, rakish and sensuous and rivalled a new Cadillac for street appeal. And as a dream car it had a special quality: the Cadillac was the car for the man who bought his dream; the hot-rod was the car for the person who built his own.

THE LATE FIFTIES

Years of chrome and fins, hot-rods, horsepower, teenage rock 'n' roll rebellion and styling gone mad

In 1955 the brand new American movie idol James Dean died in a sports car wreck in California, Elvis Presley smoked his way into adolescent hearts with *Heartbreak Hotel* and Chevrolet gave power to the people with a new OHV V8 that ended thirty years of hot-rod performance supremacy by the V8 Ford. The Corvette, the Thunderbird, the Impala, the Plymouth Fury and the Chrysler 300 answered the perennial teenagers' dream of fast cars, hot music and freedom.

IN 1955, Elvis Presley was a fast-rising star of a new form of pop music that would launch an undeclared war between adults and American teenagers. It was the year Joe DiMaggio was elected to the Baseball Hall of Fame and the year Chrysler joined Cadillac and Lincoln in the horsepower race. It was also the year James Dean died. And it was the year that the new Chevrolet V8 deposed Ford as the king of popular-priced performance cars and changed the automotive balance of power.

The flathead V8 that had given Ford the performance lead over Chevrolet in 1932 was long overdue for retirement when Ford decided to go ahead and replace it with a modern, overhead-valve V8 in 1954. Dodge had introduced an overhead-valve V8 in 1953 and Plymouth got one in 1955. But the Chevy V8 that appeared in 1955 was more efficient than either the Ford or Plymouth versions. The Chevy engine was lighter, more compact and produced more power per pound and more power per cubic inch than any other engine on the market.

In one model year, the new V8 moved Chevrolet from the economy family-car field into the performance-car world and at the same time made it king. The big news, however, was not that Chevrolet suddenly had the performance edge over Ford and Plymouth but that the low-priced three, led by Chevrolet, rivalled the performance of Cadillac, Lincoln and Chrysler. A luxury car no longer guaranteed highway superiority. A Cadillac driver risked losing a contest with a Chevrolet V8, a radical shift in the social order of an auto-oriented society. To borrow and paraphrase a slogan from the Beatles (who themselves borrowed it from the street argot of the sixties), the Chevy V8 gave power to the people. From 1955 onward, economy cars got faster and luxury cars got heavier. The high-performance Chrysler 300 introduced in 1955 may have been the fastest American production car until the end of the decade, but the focus of the horse-power-performance war unmistakably shifted from the top to the bottom of the market.

The engine alone would not have remade the Chevrolet image without the glamorous new package it was wrapped in. Chevy had fallen behind Ford in styling when Ford went to a modern, angular shape in 1952. The Chevy model change for 1953 was a new

America's Number 1 Road Car...

look, but it fell far short of Ford in glamour and appeal. The shape of the 1955 Chevy, however, was as successful as the engine. It was an immediate sensation on the market, and it still looked as good thirty years later as it had then. With clean, angular lines in the same basic rectangle shape as Ford and Plymouth, Chevrolet had a more elegant, sensuous look than either. The front and rear fenders formed a continuous horizontal line with a graceful shoulder turn-up behind the door that suggested the lush contour of the Cadillac Coupe de Ville, but in a subtlety of balanced proportion that was pure design eloquence.

Once Chevrolet had adopted V8 power as an

1955 Chevrolet Bel Air
The V8 gave GM's economy line unexpected performance parity with the luxury Cadillac and Oldsmobile lines. The 1955 and 1956 Chevrolet V8 was as quick off the line as any sedan sold in America. Now the average American could afford a car with the luxury of high performance.

option to the six, it was an all-out, no-holds-barred performance car. The standard 265 cubic-inch V8 available in all models was rated at 162hp at 4400 rpm. But an option called Power-Pak boosted the engine output to 180hp, and in 1956 a four-barrel carb 'Turbo-Fire' option put out 205hp, with an even wilder dual four-barrel carb set-up rated at 225hp. GM called the new Chevy V8 models 'The Hot Ones' and it was no idle boast. The 205hp and 225hp Chevys easily humiliated the standard Cadillac of that year. In 1957, Chevys got even hotter.

Surprisingly, the V8 Chevys were actually lighter than the six-cylinder versions of the same car, because

CHEVROLET 1955

CHEVROLET

PRODUCT VAN
GENERAL MOTORS

Left: 1955 Chevrolet
Below and right: **1957 Chevrolet Bel Air**
From 1955 on, Chevrolet offered glamour and power in the same proportion as luxury cars did – at far lower cost. Though luxury levels and styling indulgence were somewhat less marked, the performance distinction vanished altogether. The ability to out-perform with speed and power had long been an accepted feature of luxury cars. The Chevrolet eliminated that difference, and the so-called 'economy cars' were rapidly evolving into performance vehicles that could out-run anything on the road.

of the lightweight construction of the new engine. At 3230 pounds, the V8 Bel Air hardtop coupe was almost 1200 pounds lighter than the 4400-pound Cadillac two-door Coupe de Ville and had more power per pound than the Cadillac Eldorado. Though Cadillac continually raised its power output through the fifties with engine modifications and displacement increases, the power-to-weight ratio actually widened in Chevrolet's favour as the Chevy gained power and the Cadillac gained weight.

Road & Track magazine said the 225hp 1956 Chevrolet could out-accelerate any production car in the United States. That may have been an overstatement in light of the mighty Chrysler 300B, the 340hp luxury hot-rod two-door hardtop convertible coupe which outdid both Chevrolet and Cadillac in the power-per-pound ratio. But the Chrysler 300 was a very expensive, limited-production model that sold only 1100 units, while Chevrolet sold several hundred thousand V8 models in 1956.

Before the end of the year, Chevy V8s had been pulled from wrecked Chevrolets by hot-rodders, who put them in vintage Ford roadsters in place of the flathead V8s. Hot-rod Fords of the early thirties powered by souped-up Chevy V8s were faster than Cadillac or Olds V8-powered rods because the Chevrolet engine put out more power per pound. The new engine was ideally suited to racing and very quickly found its way into the world of modified sports cars on

the road-racing circuit, where with a brief upset by Ford and the Cobra, it remained the dominant power-plant for over three decades.

Because of the special attraction speed and performance had for teenagers, the new V8 immediately shifted Chevrolet into the forefront as the new American dream .car. Adult Americans may have continued to wish for the prestige of a Cadillac, a Lincoln or a Chrysler Imperial, but Chevrolet had clearly won the heart of young America. The 1956 Chevrolet styling was a further improvement on the 1955 lines, refining and extending the concept into an even more effective treatment. Slightly more angular,

Above: 1956 Cadillac Coupe de Ville
Right: 1956 Oldsmobile 88
American car styling reached a peak of handsome bigness in the middle of the fifties. The shape of the fifties 'might is right' was perfectly expressed by Cadillac and Oldsmobile.

more decorative and at the same time authoritative-looking, the 1956 Chevrolet was a styling triumph. Later models would update the concept and subsequent ones would change it, but none would surpass it in aesthetic balance and eye-pleasing line.

Unfortunately, Chevrolet, like all of General Motors, was in the grip of the styling-change frenzy encouraged by Harley Earl, who was apparently unwilling to let a good thing alone. The 1956 Chevrolet was replaced by a completely restyled car in 1957 – which was replaced by an all-new car in 1958 – which was replaced by another all-new Chevrolet in 1959. This lunacy, the ultimate expression of Earl's concept of

'dynamic obsolescence', abated in 1960. But the halt came several years too late to prevent Chevrolet's best styling from being swept out by garish overstatement that bordered on the obscene.

The performance excitement of the Chevrolet V8s burned even hotter in the 1955 and 1956 Corvette, the Chevrolet two-seat sports car first introduced in 1953. Designed as 'a young man's car', the Corvette had originally offered only the economy six-cylinder engine with Powerglide automatic transmission. The V8 was offered as a Corvette power option in 1955 and became the standard and only engine available from 1956 onwards. The Corvette got a face-lift and more power in 1956, and in 1959 received a four-speed synchromesh transmission, like the gearboxes in expensive European sports cars.

The Corvette was America's sports car, a genuine challenge to Jaguar, the Mercedes-Benz 300SL, Ferrari and Aston Martin as high-performance rulers of the road. But most Americans had never seen a European sports car, and for many the Corvette was the answer to a question that had not been asked. Corvette sales

Overleaf: 1957 Oldsmobile 88
Oldsmobile carried the long, low, swoopy look of luxury and power in every line. With every model change the Oldsmobile got longer and lower and wider in a design philosophy of overkill that continually called for more curves, longer lines, more chrome and bigger fins.

1958 Chevrolet Corvette

No other car since the war had come before the American public with so much raw appeal to the appetite for excitement than the Corvette. While the Ford Thunderbird offered sporty luxury, the Corvette was directed at the enthusiast who wanted performance before comfort. The Corvette got off to a shaky start and sold in such small numbers it was almost still-born, but by 1958 the styling had matured and the performance was a revelation in an American production car.

were only a trickle in 1955 and 1956, and just marginally better in 1957. In 1958, after the introduction of fuel injection in the fourth year of the V8, Corvette sales were slightly over 9000 out of a total of 1 240 000 Chevrolets. There was no mystery to the Corvette's low sales. The Corvette had less than half the passenger space of regular Chevrolets and cost almost twice as much. At $4400 fully loaded compared to $2800 for a comparably equipped 1958 Chevrolet Bel Air Impala, the Corvette was creeping up on Cadillac price territory — you could buy a Cadillac Series 62 two-door hardtop coupe for $5000. The Corvette was simply too much money for most of the people who wanted to buy one.

Unfulfilled desire, of course, is the essence of dream cars and always has been. Cars people buy and drive every day are not dream cars because unattainability is part of the dream. Dream cars are vehicles of fantasy, with some of the wild magic quality of an exotic jungle cat – like the Corvette. It was that kind of car: handsome, beautiful to some, tempting, tantalizing, glamorous, intimidating and not at all practical. It was a dreamer's car in an automotive era when dreams were being rewritten yearly.

Between 1955 and 1960 the horsepower race heated to such intensity that performance records barely had time to register before they were broken, then broken again as engines grew larger and more powerful every model year. American automobile

1958 Chevrolet Impala
By 1958, Chevrolet was showing the symptoms of the design excess and annual restyling frenzy that would drag the best of Detroit auto styling down into a wallow of bad taste. The dual headlights were the beginning, together with massive layers of chrome and double accents of every contour.

engines of the late fifties saw more concentrated performance development than at any time save for the production of World War II aircraft engines. With the Detroit V8, it was an all-out battle for the street-performance title while America's auto-makers pretended not to be involved in producing speed. Yet while Ford, Plymouth, Dodge, Chevrolet, Pontiac and Chrysler raised and called each other in power increases every season, the Corvette continued to be the only American car dedicated totally to performance. By 1958 the Corvette was beating Jaguar and Mercedes-Benz and challenging Ferrari on the road courses of sports-car racing, furthering the legend-in-the-making of a car that could whip other cars costing three or four times as much.

Chevrolet, meanwhile, was developing into an all-out street-racing machine as the competition with Ford and Plymouth raged. The Detroit Big Three were battling on the drag strip, the stock-car racing circuit and the street, with engines of a size and power output that would have been unimaginable a few years earlier. The milestone 265 cubic-inch Chevy V8 had been enlarged to 283 cubic inches in 1957, then replaced by a 348 cubic-inch performance engine in 1958 which was enlarged to 409 cubic inches in 1961 and stretched out to 427 cubic inches in 1967. Ford and Chrysler escalated their hot-engine size and output as rapidly as GM and there seemed no let-up in sight.

Chevrolet gained another jump on Ford and

Plymouth with the introduction of the Impala line in 1958, launching a model series that would be one of the best sellers ever. The 1958 Chevy Bel Air Impala was the final stage of styling development of the classic 1955 shape. After that it was a brand-new body and a downhill ride for styling. The purity of line of the earlier Chevys was already marred by the bloat and excess curves of the 1958 model, with overstyling accented by slabs of chrome. Still, it was a strikingly handsome car, and overstyled and overstated or not, it was an unqualified success. No one had said Americans disliked

1957 Chevrolet Nomad Station Wagon
The true automotive symbol of the American lifestyle, the station wagon was shaped and styled like a sedan with lots of space in the back for the family. The Nomad blended utility with the flash of fifties fins, two-tone styling and pizzazz.

overstatement or were necessarily put off by poor taste. The design produced by Harley Earl's styling department may have been a shade garish and vulgar, but it was exactly what the public wanted.

It was hard to keep up with the changes in the American auto market in the second half of the fifties. Every model of each car line vied with every other for first place in styling, performance and all-out glamour. Plymouth moved full speed ahead in 1955 with a smooth, angular rectangle shape designed by Virgil Exner, a GM stylist under Harley Earl until 1939, then

1957 Chrysler New Yorker and Windsor
Chief stylist Virgil Exner gave the Chrysler family a new look with a clean, sweeping fin line from front fender to tail. Modestly called the '100 million dollar look', the winged fender line gave Chrysler styling parity with General Motors. The Windsor and New Yorker were a fresh design concept of angles, planes and horizontal edges replacing traditional rounded curves.

Chrysler

presents the finest cars in its history...

★ THE NEW YORKER

★ THE WINDSOR

Glamorous is *the* word for it! Glamorous in the originality of its design—in the exclusive beauty of its new shape of motion. Here is a perfectly balanced design with the look and feel of motion in every eye-pleasing line.

The body is low, yet there is generous headroom, spacious front and rear compartments. Its long, low, flowing lines and the intentionally reserved use of chrome give it a distinctive dignity no other fine car can equal.

The Chrysler Line for 1957 includes two models

and nine smart body styles. The Chrysler New Yorker, long recognized as one of the truly fine cars, offers the sedan—the two-door hardtop—the four-door hardtop—the convertible coupe—and the Town and Country Wagon.

Next in line is the smart, new Chrysler Windsor with four beautiful body types; the sedan—the two-door hardtop—the four-door hardtop—and the Windsor Town and Country Wagon.

Your dealer will be pleased to help you make your selection.

...the most glamorous cars in a generation

1957 Plymouth Fury
A special performance edition aimed at the heart of young America, the Fury was an immediate success. Though only a tiny number were produced, the Plymouth factory hot-rod was one of the prime dream cars of a generation.

head of styling for Studebaker until he moved to Chrysler in 1949. Chrysler had lagged behind in styling in the early fifties, staying with a conservative, rounded shape long after that had been outmoded by GM and Ford. Exner was entrusted with bringing Chrysler into mainstream styling with the 1955 models, and the healthy sales for that year and the year after indicate that he succeeded.

Exner's new look for Plymouth was composed of acute angles, planes and horizontal edges instead of rounded curves, with a massive, sweeping tailfinned

profile for De Soto and Chrysler which was modestly called the '100 million-dollar look'. In 1957, the Chrysler line-up got another stylistic revamp that gave the whole family the most impressive, massive-finned fender line yet seen on an American car. Succeeding models would be as overstated and overdone as the competition at other car-makers, with excess lavished on top of excess. But the 1957 Chrysler was a styling triumph.

The highlight of the line was the high-performance 300C, a special limited-production edition introduced in 1955 (the '300' originally represented the horse-power rating of the 331 cubic-inch engine; power was up to 375hp in 1957 from an engine punched out to 392 inches but the '300' designation remained). The Chrysler V8 had been introduced in 1951 with 180hp, for one year the most powerful American car engine, until Cadillac upped engine power to 190hp in 1952 and 210hp in 1953, while Chrysler left its power output the same. Coming from behind in the horse-power race, Chrysler caught up with a vengeance in 1955. The base version of the 331 cubic-inch V8, nicknamed 'hemi-head' for the hemispherical con-figuration of the combustion chambers, was rated at 250hp. That outdid Lincoln (205hp in 1954, 225hp in 1955) and equalled the 250hp standard Cadillac engine that year. The 300 Series Chrysler hardtop coupe

powered by a souped-up hemi-head with two four-barrel carbs had the highest horsepower rating of any production car in the world, Ferrari included.

The potential of the 331 cubic-inch Chrysler hemi had just been tapped. It was bored out to 354 cubic inches for 1956 and the power of the 300 engine upped to 355hp. In 1957 the engine size was enlarged to 392 cubic inches and the power upped to 390hp. The 300 series changed Chrysler's image as the small-block V8 changed Chevrolet's. The limited-production 300 Series Chrysler letter cars, beginning with B in 1956 and going on up the alphabet each model year, was a prestige image-builder at the top of the line.

1958 Chrysler 300D
Powered by the legendary 'hemi-head' V8, the 300D was a factory hot-rod. The 300D, like the earlier 300C and the later 300E, had specially tuned suspension and heavy-duty brakes. The gut-wrenching torque produced the highest top speed of any American production car.

The 300 Series was a blazing performance success. The 300 won stock car championship titles in 1955, clocked 139 mph at Daytona Beach in 1956 for a world passenger car speed record and set the fastest qualifying lap record at Daytona International Speedway in 1954, 1955 and 1956. The 1957 Chrysler 300C, third in the letter-car series (which came only in two-door hardtop or convertible versions) was the fastest and most powerful production car in the country for the third year in a row.

Though street-rodders favoured the Chevrolet V8 for its lightness and superb breathing capability at high rpm, the Chrysler hemi-head V8 became the King

Previous pages and left:
**1959 Plymouth
Sport Fury**
The car featured in the American gothic horror movie *Christine* (top right) from the Stephen King novel was a 1958 Fury. Plymouth's challenge to Chevrolet for domination of street hot-rod performance, the Fury was finned, chromed, powerful and fast.

Kong of unlimited drag racing. The Chrysler hemi powered the AA Fuel dragsters that set absolute acceleration and top-speed records in the quarter mile in the late fifties, sixties and seventies. An evolutionary descendant of that engine is still the undisputed champion of unlimited drag race competition more than thirty years later. The car it powered – the 300C – was a dream car for millions of Americans. At $5000 it was far too costly for most people, but no more expensive than the standard 1957 Cadillac and held the distinction of being one of the world's fastest cars.

The Plymouth Fury was a modest-priced performance counterpart to the 300C. Introduced as a division of the Belvedere series in 1956, the Fury was a teenage hot-rodder's dream. It came only in a special shade of white, with gold trim, dual exhaust, special wheel covers and tyres and a 240hp engine, handily outpointing the hottest Chevrolet V8 in 1956. In 1957 an even hotter Fury was available boasting two four-barrel carbs and 290hp.

Plymouth came out with a brand-new body in 1957, sporting rakish tailfins and a massive cross-hatched grille with horizontally placed quad headlights. The new Plymouths were dramatically lower, wider and longer – so much so that they escaped the economy-car look altogether. The 1957 Plymouth was a big car

with big-car styling and the look was so popular that sales climbed almost 50 per cent, from 453 000 to 655 000, knocking Buick out of third place in the sales league. For 1958 the Fury engine came even hotter, with a 305hp 'Golden Commando' 'Dual Fury' engine option. As a car dedicated to the maximum thrill of absolute performance, the Plymouth Fury appealed to the taste for serious adventure. For millions of American teenagers, the 1957 or 1958 Plymouth Fury was the most desirable car on the road. The gothic-horror novelist Stephen King was sufficiently inspired by the mystique of the Fury to cast it as the lead in his best-seller *Christine* and the movie derived from it – the story of a demonically possessed 1958 Plymouth Fury.

The unchecked horsepower and performance race which so delighted American youth was viewed with alarm by many adults who were already worried about the cultural ravages being wrought by the dread new pop music called rock-and-roll. Part of the battle between the generations was over sex. Grown-ups were against it (outside of marriage) and teenagers were for it. Cars and rock-and-roll made sex easier, or so parents believed. They were probably right. And fast, glamorous cars made everything worse.

Facing a tide of public and government criticism of the spiralling speed and power of American cars, the

Automobile Manufacturers' Association (AMA) agreed in 1957 to end factory-supported racing as a brake on the performance escalation. The horsepower race continued, however, with Lincoln topping the ranks in 1958 with a special 3x2 carb option of the 430 cubic-inch V8 that raised power from the standard 375hp to 400hp. Even with 400hp, the 1958 Lincoln was too heavy to be fast and speed was no longer seriously cultivated as part of the image. Ford had a better image car; its name was Thunderbird.

Introduced in 1955 as a smart, sporty lightweight, the Thunderbird broke fresh ground in American car styling. It sectioned and compressed the rectangular look of the 1955 Ford into a thinner, lower, more graceful shape, a shape that was and is one of the prettiest American auto designs ever produced. In its first three model years, the Thunderbird was strictly a two-seater in the sports-car image of the Corvette. But the Corvette, which started out as an odd-looking two-seater with a six-cylinder engine and automatic transmission, had faltered and almost foundered at the start; only a major styling revamp and a V8 engine eventually helped Corvette take hold of the enthusiastic

Above: 1955 Ford Thunderbird
Below: 1956 Ford Thunderbird
A sporty car for the person with money who wanted to think young, the Thunderbird arrived in 1955 with a new image which became an immediate market success.

but narrow performance market. By contrast, the Thunderbird hit the market styled to perfection, with a powerful V8, and did spectacularly well for a brand-new, limited-capacity car, with 16 000 sales in 1955, its first market year, compared with Corvette's meagre 700 sales in its third year. The Thunderbird was nicknamed T-Bird and quickly became an image of success and the American good life.

Though the T-Bird roughly matched the Chevy Corvette in power and performance options in 1955 and 1956, it had a softer image. Comfort and personal luxury were emphasized over speed and power to

Above and right: **1957 Ford Thunderbird**
Graceful and subtle in an era of massive excess and overstyling, the T-Bird was a classic in its own time. The shape stayed unspoiled through the first three model years as the car's popularity grew. The Thunderbird was a pure American sports style that owed nothing to European influences. It was a brilliantly successful blend of luxury and prestige with a sporty image. The Thunderbird was a statement of what Americans wanted their lives to be.

tailor a sporty car for the person with money who wanted to look young. In 1958 the T-Bird became a four-seater, giving up all pretence to being a sports car, and sales shot up. The four-seat T-Bird followed the evolutionary model for most American cars except the Corvette: it grew bigger, wider, longer and heavier for 1958, with an enormous 800-pound weight gain over 1957. Sales of the bigger, heavier and cushier T-Bird jumped from 21 000 in 1957 to 37 000 in 1958 and 67 000 in 1959.

The classic T-Bird of 1955-7 had a romantic purity of style and concept that appealed to millions who could not afford it, an irony which was true of most dream cars, American or not. The Thunderbird was part of the lyrics of more than one pop record of the late fifties, and played the dream car driven by the beautiful, unattainable blonde siren in the movie *American Graffiti*.

The dream cars of this period, with their hot engines, high performance, and ice-cream sundae styling, seemed aimed directly at American teenagers. The Plymouth Fury, the Chevrolet Impala, the Chrysler 300C, the Pontiac Bonneville and the Corvette made

lasting imprints as vehicles of desire for the high-school generation of the fifties. Few teenagers could afford to buy those cars new or even a year or two old, but millions vowed to earn enough to drive an Impala, a Bonneville or a Fury when they were older.

The wild, exciting cars reflected a shift in cultural and marketing values towards a new generation coming of age in post-war America, the so-called 'Baby Boomers' born during or right after World War II, with a taste for the new and different. American teenagers had fallen completely for the threatening, rebellious, roughneck

THE CAR *EVERYONE* WOULD LOVE TO OWN

Above: **1959 Ford Thunderbird**
Left and right: **1960 Ford Thunderbird**
In 1958, the T-Bird shed all pretence of sportiness and excitement for the added convenience of rear seats. The new four-passenger T-Bird was bigger, heavier, slower and less imaginatively styled. Weight and added bulk blunted the crisp lines and dulled the taut edges of the styling of the two-seater. A sporty car for the sporty family, the redesign of the car was marketing genius, immediately enhancing sales success as buyers were given what they really wanted: a sporty image with living-room comfort and convenience.

Previous pages and left:
1959 Chevrolet Impala
By 1959, the spreading wave of terminal bad taste had turned America's best-looking cars into gargoyles. Like mistakes from some Frankenstein monster design lab, the cars of 1959 and 1960 vied with each other in ugliness and garish caricature. The Chevrolet Impala somehow got its fins turned sideways, perhaps due to a mistake in the oven, and no-one noticed until it was dry. Fins and useless vents are everywhere.

Right: 1958 Edsel Citation
One year ahead of the general wave of ugliness, the Edsel managed to sink in its own wake.

sensuality of Elvis Presley and the other new rockers – Jerry Lee Lewis, Carl Perkins, Chuck Berry, Gene Vincent and Little Richard. There were new excitements on the movie screen too. Marlon Brando played a brooding, rebellious motorcycle rider in *The Wild One*, James Dean a tragically misunderstood teen in *Rebel Without a Cause*, and Elvis Presley a rebellious Southern singing hot-rodder in any number of Elvis movies. They had given the young knife-wielding leather-jacketed hood a national image and rebellion was in the air.

Stock-car racing and drag racing boomed as major motor sports in the late fifties, both of them outlaw activity set to rules on the track: stock-car racing had roots in Southern backwoods moonshine whiskey-running and drag racing was born out of two-car urban asphalt automotive stoplight shoot-outs. Both sports drew millions of ordinary Americans to watch cars that looked and sounded just like the ones they drove. Both sports celebrated the affair between Americans and their cars that was never more passionate than in the late fifties.

Not everyone loved new American cars. Some thought they were brash, arrogant displays of chrome, fins, enamelled sheet-metal and excess power in a decadent extravaganza of size and ostentation. In the

73

1958 Edsel Citation
So ugly it deserved to be destroyed on sight, the Edsel remains a monument to poor planning, bad design and industrial arrogance at its height.

popular book *The Insolent Chariots*, author John Keats satirized American cars as mechanical pets that had taken over their masters. President Dwight D. Eisenhower joined the criticism, complaining from the White House on behalf of the consumer that Detroit was not giving the American public the cars it wanted. American Motors president George Romney ridiculed the cars of the Big Three as motorized juke-boxes, and large numbers of buyers agreed with him. In fact, 1958 was a disastrous sales year for the Big Three. American Motors, with its compact economy Rambler American, was the only company to increase its sales, and it did even better business in 1959.

The AMA ban on factory-supported auto racing had ended official factory teams in drag racing and stock-car racing, but the support continued unofficially and production-line cars made for the street were more powerful than ever before. As cars got bigger, design seemed to spin out of control, with style sacrificed to change for the sake of change and taste almost

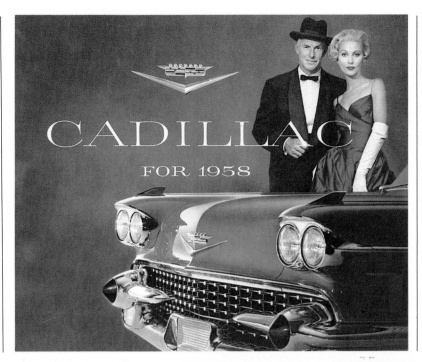

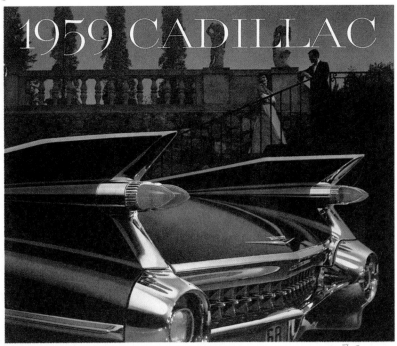

Top left: **1958 Cadillac**
Above: **1959 Cadillac**
As ugly as it was, the Edsel is bland next to the screaming insanity of the 1959 Cadillac, widely acknowledged as the ugliest car ever produced. An exercise in excess, exaggerated art deco with baroque embellishment of gross and deformed shapes, the 1959 Cadillac stands out as the worst example of unrestrained bad taste in American design history. Chrysler spread garish ugliness throughout its model lines. So did Ford. Even the self-righteous American Motors Corporation fell under the sway of hideous fins and repulsive chrome on top of chrome. After 1959, American car design could only get better.

The unrestrained sweep of tailfins and a mouthful of chrome grillework at the front typified the Cadillac look of the late fifties and early sixties. The statement was clear: more is more, bigger is better, fins are fun and chrome is beautiful. The Series 62 was a mammoth 18.5 feet long, weighed 4600 pounds and boasted 325hp from a 390 cubic-inch V8. Standard equipment included power brakes, power steering, automatic transmission, dual reversing lights, windshield washer, dual speed wipers and remote control outside rearview mirrors. As powerful as the Series 62 was, Cadillac's performance image was declining. The dual exhaust and triple carburettor option of previous years was discontinued, with single exhaust and a single four-barrel carburettor the only choice available.

completely obliterated in favour of the proposition that bigger is better, fins are fun, chrome is beautiful and more chrome is even better.

The high aesthetic standard reached by GM, Ford and Chrysler in 1957 gave way to excess and baroque ugliness as the styling divisions of all three auto-makers seemed to go insane. In 1958 Ford delivered the Edsel, widely considered the ugliest car of all time, except for the 1958 Buick, the 1959 Oldsmobile, the 1959 Chrysler Imperial, the 1959 Chevy Impala and the 1959 Cadillac, which stand today as monuments to bad taste. It was a time of styling run amok in unchecked mutations of fins upon fins, chrome upon chrome with all semblance of

proportion and spatial harmony abandoned. No corporate styling division came through this madness unscathed. American Motors contributed to the pollution with Rambler Rebels and Ambassadors as over-chromed and ugly as any. Only the Corvette and the sensible, clean-cut, Italian-accented Rambler American kept their lines and styling intact during this epidemic of ugliness and excess.

It had been a busy decade that began with jet air travel still a novelty, and ended with the Space Age under way. In a ten-year span American cars had grown in size, luxury and power to a degree beyond the imagination in 1949.

THE EARLY SIXTIES

'Route 66', the golden age of the Corvette and the escalation of the horsepower race

At the start of the Kennedy era, the Corvette ruled the road and the TV series *Route 66* was a weekly restatement of the adventure of the American dream on wheels. The horsepower race escalated with big and bigger engines in big and bigger cars, a time of excess in styling, of arrogance in motion. The AC Cobra knocked out the Corvette in one punch and the Pontiac GTO launched the muscle car era.

BY 1960 a standard Chevy, Ford or Plymouth could be ordered with more power, performance and wraparound luxury than Cadillac, Lincoln or Chrysler offered in the early fifties. In one decade the American economy car had moved so far in luxury, size, power and styling that the distinctions between the automotive classes were blurred. The 1960 Chevrolet Impala, Pontiac Bonneville, Ford Galaxy or Plymouth Fury offered power steering, power brakes, power windows, a hoice of automatic or manual transmissions, remote control outside rearview mirrors, six-way power seats, hi-fi radio, air conditioning, variable speed windshield washers and power doorlocks.

In 1950 a Chevrolet sold for $1500. By 1960 it had gained 500 pounds and grown almost a foot longer, and the price had doubled to $3000. The 1950 Chevrolet came with either a three-speed manual transmission or Powerglide. In 1960, transmission choices included two-speed Powerglide automatic or three-speed Turboglide automatic, three-speed manual, three-speed close-ratio manual, four-speed close-ratio manual, and overdrive. Instead of two engine choices for the entire model range – a 90hp six and a 105hp in 1950 – the Chevy motor menu for 1960 listed a 135hp six and no less than six V8s: a Super Turbo-Fire V8, a Ram-Jet Fuel Injection V8, a Turbo-Thrust V8, a Super Turbo-Thrust V8, a Special Turbo-Thrust V8 and a Special Super Turbo-Thrust V8, in ascending horsepower from 230hp to 315hp. Over this ten-year period, the Chevy power-to-weight ratio had increased three-fold from 34 pounds per horsepower to 11 pounds per horsepower. The 0-60 mph acceleration had been cut from around 20 seconds in 1950 to less than 7 seconds for the 1960 Chevy 348 Special Super Turbo-Thrust.

In that same decade Cadillac had almost doubled in price, grown a foot longer and put on almost 1000 pounds. The weight gain, similar to the pounds put on by Lincoln and Chrysler, reversed the pecking order of performance. Luxury cars now ruled the road in size, weight and price only, with performance superiority ceded to low-priced siblings – Chevy, Ford and Plymouth. It was not that American luxury cars had got slow: the 1960 Cadillac, Lincoln or Chrysler could easily out-accelerate the fastest European or English sedan. It was simply that Chevrolets, Fords and

Right: **1963 Chrysler 300J** In the sixties, full-size American cars engaged in a full-scale horsepower/ performance war that produced street cars with an unprecedented degree of speed. Though the economy three – Ford, Chevrolet and Plymouth – had the leading edge in performance with huge engines and relatively light weight, the luxury three piled horsepower upon horsepower to keep up. The Chrysler letter series 300 was the best of the luxury hot-rods.

1959 Ford Galaxy Skyliner
The clean, rectangular lines of the 1959 Ford were carried to the extreme of a rectracable hard-top convertible called the Skyliner.

1964 Pontiac Bonneville
No Porsche, no Ferrari, Lamborghini or Mercedes Benz sold in the United States in the eighties can better the acceleration times of the hottest Detroit supercars of the early sixties. The fastest cars, such as the Pontiac Bonneville, featured speed over style, horsepower over comfort. The time of the most dramatic advances in engine performance was a time of unimaginative design, with bland shapes and conservative lines. The supercars of the early sixties were crude machines which made considerable sacrifice for absolute performance. They were never popular with the average buyer, but they were cars of lasting reputation.

Plymouths had mutated from utility family sedans to out-and-out street combat vehicles with the power to out-accelerate any production sports car, including Ferrari, Maserati, Porsche, Jaguar, Mercedes-Benz and Aston Martin.

This extraordinary performance was bargain-priced. On a scale of dollars-per-horsepower, the 90 horses of the $1500 1950 Chevrolet cost $16.60 each and the 160 horses of the $3400 Cadillac cost $20 each. By 1960, the price of Chevrolet power had dropped to an incredibly low $8.90 per horsepower in one of the bargain power sales of all time. The rates were the same from Ford and Plymouth. It was a horsepower race out of control, and it got more so. In 1962, advertised horsepower spilled over the 400 mark, with 409 for Chevrolet, 405 for Ford and 405 for Plymouth. Those figures dropped the weight-to-power ratios down to 8.5:1, and cut the horsepower cost to $8.55 a horse.

The performance of those monster-motor street-racing cars defies imagination. No Porsche, Ferrari, Lamborghini or Mercedes-Benz sold in the United States in the 1980s can approach the acceleration times of the hottest Detroit supercars of the early 1960s. But with eyeball-flattening performance available at the local economy-car dealer, what was there to dream about? The Ford, Chevy, and Plymouth supercars were all speed and no style; they had no special looks to inspire dreams. Most buyers did not care for the thunderous performance, settling for standard engines and spending the extra cash on a special luxury interior package or on installing a better AM-FM radio.

The car that kept the American dream on wheels in the early sixties was the Corvette. Still an undiluted adventure vehicle for the romantic, the Corvette reached a high point of all-American good looks with the quad-headlight, recessed side-cove styling of 1961 and 1962. The popular fuel-injection option gave the Corvette the technological edge on other American cars and for 1962 power was a whopping 360hp from 327 fuel-injected cubic inches. The fuel-injected Corvette, known as the 'fuelie', could be beaten in straight-line acceleration by the Impala 348 SS or Ford's Interceptor police-engine special, but the Corvette was good for more than straight lines. America's only sports car could carve up a winding road, as long as the surface was smooth, without losing its poise or going off the road. The Corvette, as the ads tried to explain, was more than an exciting car; it was an exciting way of life.

1961 Chevrolet Corvette
The Corvette in the sixties was more than an exciting car. It was an exciting way of life. As the star of the smash hit TV series *Route 66*, the Corvette crystallized a vision of romantic highway wandering that had long been part of the American dream. The Corvette was a car for escape into pure adventure.

If you thought your life was dull, why not buy a Corvette and change it?

Buying a Corvette took a strong sense of adventure and a healthy bank balance. At $4000 in 1961, the Corvette was an expensive car. It was an irony with the Corvette, as with most powerful sports cars, that most of the people who wanted it most couldn't afford it and most of the people who did have the money preferred something more conservative.

In the early 1960s, millions of Americans lived the Corvette adventure vicariously through the popular weekly TV series *Route 66*. The show starred two footloose young men roving the backroads in a red

1963 Corvette Sting Ray

Corvette was spared the model-change mania of the late fifties that spoiled other car designs. America's one true sports car stayed free of major styling changes until 1963, when a radical redesign called the Sting Ray was introduced. Unlike so many other cars whose names promised excitement but failed to deliver, the Corvette Sting Ray was the real thing. Faster, with better handling than any other American car, the Corvette Sting Ray finally brought the American sports car to world-class quality in engineering and performance. From the fast but crude versions that preceded it, the Corvette evolved in the Sting Ray to

a slick, sophisticated sports car that was more in the manner of the European *gran turismo* sports car than Corvette's American hot-rod ancestors.

Corvette convertible, travelling the American heartland, meeting crises in small towns, solving problems and moving on. The show was adventure on the move, an unknown horizon at the journey's end and a fast, exciting car to travel in. The image of a red Corvette pounding down a two-lane blacktop to the driving jazz beat of the *Route 66* theme crystallized a vision of romantic highway wandering that had been part of the American dream since the beginning.

The 1962 Corvette was the last year of a body style in production since 1958. As a special GM model, the Corvette was spared the model-change mania that infected other lines. But a major change came in 1963

with the new Sting Ray, a restyle so extensive that it was practically a new car. The new body enveloped a motor, drive-train and transmission package re-engineered to provide equal front-to-rear weight distribution, an ideal balance for a performance car. The body came in both convertible and detachable hardtop as before, but also as a fastback coupe, which was new. The fastback coupe was a flawless automotive sculpture unsullied by the gimmicks or chrome gewgaws that marred so many Detroit cars. Though perhaps lacking in the openly macho styling excitement of the 1962 Corvette, the Sting Ray looked like a grown-up sports car, which it was. The new Corvette

Left: **1964 Corvette Sting Ray**
Right: **1963 Buick Riviera**
The fresh, clean and elegant styling of the Sting Ray and the Buick Riviera reflected the refined taste of new GM head stylist William Mitchell. As successor to Harley Earl, Mitchell ushered in a new era of design excellence. The Buick Riviera marked a high point that showed how good an American auto design can be. But like the bold, advanced look of the 1962 Dodge Dart, the Buick Riviera was a look not destined to last. The clean lines of the Riviera were blunted and dulled with each model change, losing the unique quality that made the car a classic in its own time.

bore the imprint of the new GM head stylist William Mitchell, successor to Harley Earl, and the Sting Ray was a styling triumph. The shape was a clean, knife-edged envelope, with a sloped roofline that had the inevitability of flawless design. It looked so right it seemed obvious that any other configuration would have looked wrong, and the split rear window gave the 1963 and 1964 fastbacks instant classic appeal. Later Corvettes would go faster but none were more beautiful than the Sting Ray.

As GM styling slipped the chains of Harley Earl, the compact 1961 Valiant and the down-size 1962 Dodge Dart were Chrysler design ventures away from the fins and slab-tails and chrome bucket mouths. The Valiant and the Dart were taut, sharp-lined European-accented designs composed of angles and planes with almost no curves. Chrysler named it the 'Forward Flair' look and called the Dart the 'new, lean breed of Dodge' because it was smaller and several hundred pounds lighter than the full-size Dodge it replaced. But this bold, radical styling failed in the market. The lean breed of Dodge was put on ice after only one model year and replaced by a full-size Dodge with fins and massive slabs of chrome; putting Chrysler back into the morass of styling mediocrity that was the order of the day in Detroit.

The 1963 Buick Riviera was a GM counter to the Thunderbird, and one of Detroit's best efforts at a car with a European *gran turismo* accent. The Riviera was a special-edition Buick produced under the direction of Bill Mitchell and promoted as 'America's bid for a great new international classic'. Sharp-edged, with flush, full curves and what could honestly be called 'graceful bulk', to use Harley Earl's description, the Buick Riviera appeared elegant and fast – as it was supposed to.

Buick advertised a 'specially tuned' suspension for the Riviera, which came with a 325hp 401 cubic-inch V8, with a 340hp option available with two four-barrel carburettors in 1964. The most expensive Buick at $4340, the Riviera sold an impressive 40 000 units in 1963, its first year on the market. It kept its basic shape through 1965, retaining its identity as a sleek, refined, well-engineered car with rare beauty for a Detroit sedan. The Riviera was an outstanding example of grace and style. Though styling modifications gradually degenerated it into an over-laden, exaggerated shape that stamped it as just another Buick sedan by 1970, the original edition remains unsurpassed as an eye-pleaser. The Riviera is one of the very few American cars that actually achieved the advertised goal of becoming a classic in its own time.

The Shelby Cobra was neither sophisticated nor beautiful. It was brutal, crude and violent. While the Corvette Sting Ray and the Riviera took balanced and refined approaches to performance engineering, the Cobra was an uncompromising assault vehicle designed to crush existing sports car performance records. It succeeded. Born of a brawny Ford V8 transplanted into a skinny, lightweight English sports car chassis, the Cobra was several hundred pounds lighter than the Corvette and equally powerful. The simple arithmetic of low weight and high power produced a car that could whip the Corvette – and any other car – on its own terms.

The Cobra was the creation of Carroll Shelby, a retired racing champion with a rare gift for promotion and marketing. A smooth-talking, good-looking Texan living in Los Angeles, Shelby cajoled the Ford Motor Company into supplying engines, and the makers of the British AC sports roadsters into supplying the cars. An American V8 in a lightweight sports car – lighter than the Corvette – was not a new idea, but Shelby made it an unprecedented success. The AC Cobra was the world's fastest production car in an age of Detroit production sedans with more speed than had ever before been put on the road. Twenty-three years later, the acceleration times of the Cobra stand un-

broken, a monument to street performance that has no immediate challenger.

The Cobra styling was originally the work of an English stylist named John Tojeiro whose design for the AC Ace closely resembled a racing Ferrari of the early fifties. The shape was soft and flowing with restrained curves, swooping front fenders and a snub tail. The car was a joint project of Shelby American and the Ford Motor Company, which got credit through a nameplate on the front fender with the words 'Powered by Ford'. For the first two years of Cobra production the English-styled bodywork was basically unchanged and the powerplant was the 289 cubic-inch V8 that became the Mustang engine.

The Cobra 289 won races in its first season on the track, an almost unheard-of accomplishment in auto racing. In its second year, 1963, the Cobra won a national championship. In 1964 Shelby revamped the car to accommodate the big-block Ford 427, an engine powerful enough to move a full-size Ford sedan like a rocket. The performance it gave the Cobra 427 is the stuff of legend. The most famous measure of big-block Cobra performance was a test performed by *Car & Driver* magazine, in which a Cobra 427 accelerated from a standstill to 100 mph – and came to a full stop – in less than 14 seconds.

1965 AC Cobra
The Shelby Cobra was an automotive boxing glove. Neither sophisticated nor particularly beautiful, it was rugged, violent and overwhelmingly effective. Born of a brawny American V8 transplanted into a skinny, lightweight British sports car chassis, the Cobra was a vehicle designed for assault and annihilation of all existing performance records. It succeeded. The AC Cobra was the world's fastest production car in an age of Detroit sedans that were faster than any cars ever put on the road before. Cobra acceleration times remain a performance landmark 23 years later.

Thanks to clever press releases by Carroll Shelby, the Cobra was a legend before it even reached production. The published reports, which appeared constantly once production was under way, added lustre to an already mythic automotive reputation. The Cobra fascinated journalists and readers alike, which helped it get editorial coverage unrivalled by any other car. The Cobra was the car that enthusiasts liked to talk and read about, the car journalists liked to write about. It embodied more pure excitement than any other car ever produced.

But few people experienced the excitement of the Cobra at first hand. At $8000 the Cobra 427 was almost twice the price of a Corvette and half again as expensive as a Cadillac. While the Corvette stinted on comfort and passenger accommodation for performance, the Cobra offered no accommodation. The driver and passenger merely fitted themselves into the cramped, uninsulated cockpit and got jolted with the highest-voltage thrill on wheels. Staying comfortable, keeping cool despite the stifling heat transmitted through the floorboards, or dealing with gale-force wind buffet at speed, was up to the driver and rider. The Cobra's only function was delivering speed, and that it did.

Only a few hundred Cobras were sold each year, less than one-twentieth the number of Corvettes.

1965 AC Cobra
A joint project of the Ford Motor Company and a Texan-turned-Californian named Carroll Shelby, the Cobra was a triumph of ingenuity and entrepreneurship. The idea had been tried before, but never with the success earned by the Cobra. Of all the American cars ever to go into production, the Cobra was the most uncompromised effort at realizing the dream of absolute performance.

Sales of less than a thousand cars a year would have passed almost unnoticed by the press with a lesser car, but the Cobra generated publicity as easily as it won races, and the prestige it brought Ford was immeasurable. In 1964 the Cobra won the US National Road-Racing Championship and in 1966 it defeated Ferrari and Porsche to win the World Manufacturers' Championship.

The US victory over the Chevrolet Corvette was gratifying to Ford and the World Championship even more so. But Henry Ford II had made it a personal

mission to beat Ferrari in the Le Mans 24 Hours, the longest, fastest and most prestigious sports-car race in the world. As a roadster with great looks but poor aerodynamics, the Cobra was not suited for the straight-away speeds of over 200 mph needed at Le Mans. Ford commissioned an English racing car facility to produce a Le Mans car and later hired Carroll Shelby to manage the racing team. Cobra production was shelved in favour of the Le Mans-winning Ford GT, and the last Cobra was built in 1967. Yet in just five years, the Cobra had become a legend.

The Cobra was a variation on the California hot-rodding tradition of do-it-yourself speed. Carroll Shelby had successfully applied the practices of that underground, after-hours passion of garage mechanics, metalworkers and performance-seekers to a production sports cars. By the sixties, Detroit had begun to do its own hot-rodding.

The performance wars and the horsepower race of the fifties had not slowed with the AMA ban on racing in 1957. Instead, factory support of racing had simply gone under the table and the performance ferocity of

Rock music in the sixties followed the popular fast cars. The Chevy 409 generated the song *409*. The Cobra got its own song, too, but the big hit in American car songs was the Beach Boys' tribute to the Pontiac GTO, itself the big star of hot cars of the sixties. Born in the hot-rod tradition of a big engine in a small car, the Pontiac GTO was a genuine performance car with the mass market success of a hit record.

street cars intensified. Before the Cobra hit the street or track, Chevrolet was the crowned king of street and drag racing with a 409 cubic-inch V8-powered Impala. The 406 cubic-inch Ford Galaxy was almost as fast, and so was the the 413 cubic-inch Dodge Dart. But the 1962 Chevy 409 was the fastest car on the street and got a special tribute in the form of a song by the Beach Boys entitled *409*.

The Beach Boys were a southern California pop group that put close, high vocal harmonies to a driving rock beat for a new sound that was inaccurately known as 'surf rock'. The Beach Boys sang about surfing as much as they sang about hot-rodding and dating and rock-and-roll. So did Jan & Dean, the Rondells and other sixties' groups. Pop songs had been written and sung about hot-rods before, the most famous being Chuck Berry's classic *Maybelline*. But Berry's song, like Johnny Bond's *Hot-Rod Lincoln* of 1960, was a song about a home-built hot-rod whipping a Cadillac on the road.

In the 1960s, pop music and Detroit cars shared an evolutionary shift – in opposite directions. While most pop music of the fifties consisted of songs by stylized

entertainers that came out of the songwriting mill in New York City known as 'Tin Pan Alley', the pop-rock idols of the sixties were self-taught singers and groups performing songs they had written themselves. Fifties hot-rodding was home-built cars, sixties rock was home-made songs. Yet in the sixties, Detroit was into the game of hot-rodding, and the cars celebrated by the Beach Boys, the Rondells and Jan & Dean were factory-built hot-rods instead of home-builts.

The Beach Boys' tribute to the 409 was not an outstanding piece of pop music. Nor was the Chevrolet 409 a car to fire the imagination of any but the hard-core quarter-mile racer. The full-size Chevrolet, like the full-size Ford and the full-size Plymouth, was a shape that had outgrown itself. Size was a prime asset in an automobile during the fifties when bigness meant cost, which meant status. But by 1960, imposing dimensions were taken for granted, with full vinyl interiors, padded sun-visors, two-tone upholstery and power-retractable antennas. Cars were as loaded with convenience features as they were with horsepower. The next step in dream cars would be something different.

The Pontiac GTO may not have been the first Detroit factory hot-rod, but it was the forerunner of the entire generation of pony cars that dominated the late sixties and the seventies. Like the Cobra, the GTO was a deceptively simple concept: put the hottest engine from a full-size car into a smaller car and sell it as a performance special. Oldsmobile had done this as early as 1952 with the Super 88, which was a 98 engine in an 88 car. But the Pontiac GTO went several steps beyond that Olds.

The basic car was the down-size Pontiac Tempest introduced in 1961 as the Pontiac small car. By 1964 the Tempest had put on weight and inches until it was no longer small. Pontiac called it a 'senior compact', although it was mid-size or larger. The Tempest Le Mans was a sport two-door coupe or convertible model available with a 326 cubic-inch V8 tuned to 260hp. The Tempest 326 was a fast car, but not fast enough to beat the full-size Pontiac powered by the massive 421 cubic-inch V8, or the big-inch full-size Chevy, Ford or Plymouth.

For 1964, Pontiac created a new sub-species of the Tempest Le Mans by dropping in the 389 cubic-inch V8 equipped with triple two-barrel carbs and tuned to 348hp. The GTO title was a steal from the hottest Ferrari of the day, the racing 250 GTO, in which the letters stood for *gran turismo omologato*. That meant the car had been approved for the manufacturers'

championship racing series as a production sports racer. The letters may have been pretentious on a Pontiac aimed at stoplight contests on Woodward Avenue in Detroit, but the new car was an immediate success. Once again the formula of high horsepower in a low-weight car paid off. At 3100, the Tempest GTO was 800 pounds lighter than a full-size Bonneville or Grand Prix. The weight advantage translated into a formidable performance edge which made the new GTO one of the fastest cars on the road.

The Beach Boys' *GTO* was a better song than *409* and the GTO was a better car than the Chevy. The GTO was special to American teenagers because it

1965 Pontiac GTO

With unusually subtle and understated styling for an American performance car, the Pontiac GTO was an unexpected success for Pontiac. The initials of the name were borrowed from Ferrari. Or perhaps they were simply stolen. It's unlikely Sr Ferrari was ever asked.

had clearly been designed for them. It was not a grown-up's car. Everything about it was geared to performance and the style of speed, from the name to the triple-carb engine and the special Hurst racing gear-shift lever that came standard with the also standard synchromesh gearbox.

The GTO was ready for street racing, for Van Nuys or Whittier Boulevard cruising, for driving to the car-hop restaurant on Sunset Boulevard just as it came from the showroom. The GTO brought in the age of the muscle car, another phase in the continuing performance escalation, with bigger engines going into smaller cars.

THE LATE SIXTIES

The supercar and psychedelia, the muscle car, the Beatles and the Beetle change the shape of the future

In 1965 the AC Cobra won the world car racing championship and set street speed records unbroken 23 years later. The Shelby GT-350, the GTO, the Camaro Z28 and the Dodge hemi-Charger raised street fighting to new levels of intensity as turmoil over the Vietnam war racked the American psyche. The teenage revolt turned psychedelic with the Beatles and street politics. While American car style went further into luxury, performance and image, a statement of anti-style called the Volkswagen Beetle showed a new shape for the future.

IN 1964 the Ford Mustang was launched, and it became the automotive success story of the sixties – a sporty, personal car with a look almost everyone liked at a price almost anyone could afford. When it arrived on the market, the Mustang made the covers of *Time* and *Newsweek* magazines, and it went on to outsell any other single model since the Model T. A stylish new two-door body built on the Falcon chassis, the Mustang was the right car at the right time. The marriage of sports coupe (or convertible) style with sedan comfort was a winning combination, and the graceful, understated styling was a clean break from the bulk of the full-size car.

The Mustang was a new direction in the model proliferation which, since the late fifties, had spawned endless variations of the family car. As a low-priced variant on the Thunderbird theme, it appealed to singles and young marrieds who were not interested in a family-car look. A carefully nurtured media campaign fostered the Mustang image of a spirited, stylish vehicle, with the suggestion that buying one could change a person's life for the better. The styling, developed by the studio of Ford head stylist Eugene Bordinat, was clean and rectangular with a chic look that seemed to please everyone. It was sporty without the limitations of a sports car and sexy without a high price tag.

It was inevitable in the sixties that a car as popular as the Mustang would get put to music. The song *Mustang Sally* made the pop charts in 1966; the first version was sung by the Young Rascals and later soul singer Wilson Pickett recorded it too. But while the Mustang made the charts and magazine covers with its record-shattering sales, the car stirring up the most excitement on the street was the GTO.

A success on a much smaller scale than the Mustang in 1964, the GTO got a major restyling in 1966. The new Tempest models had a 'Coke-bottle' curved fender, giving a flow to the lines that the previous year's rectangular shapes lacked. The GTO got a blacked-out grille and a hood duct with twin air-inlet scoops for a particularly business-like appearance. Like most air-intake ducts on American cars, the GTO scoops were fake. But, along with the blacked-out grille, they helped create a tough image. If the Mustang was a fun car for the young-at-heart, the GTO was a tough car intended to be taken seriously. A red insignia

1965 Mustang Fastback
The Mustang was the biggest single success story in the American automobile business since the Model T Ford. A new concept with a fresh look, the Mustang was a low-priced family-car version of the ever-successful four-seater Thunderbird. A practical, inexpensive car with a sporty image, good looks, a distinctive shape and a sharp new name, the genesis of the Mustang was as simple as making a two-door car out of a small four-door sedan. But the inspired execution, and the jazzy style that resulted, had everything to do with the Mustang's success.

1965 Mustang Fastback
The Mustang was successful in three different shapes: fastback, notchback and convertible. The varied shapes reflected the range of character the car could take on depending on engine and equipment. From a soft, comfortable economy six with automatic transmission, the Mustang was available with a snarling 289 V8, 4-speed synchromesh transmission for tyre-smoking performance. But it was the range of the image and the popularity of the looks, rather than performance, that made the Mustang so successful. Most people didn't want a performance car, but millions wanted the look of one. The Mustang had the look, with or without the performance.

behind each front wheel well, GTO lettering on the deck lid and rear fenders, and a pin-stripe outlining the belt-line identified the GTO. The thin red stripe on the high-performance Goodyears was part of the package with the rectangular parking lights in the blacked-out grille. The subtle trim announced the car as different and special without seeming obvious, though any American teenage car nut could recognize a GTO at 300 yards on a dark night, which was the way Pontiac planned it.

The image of the GTO as a serious driver's car was heightened by the standard equipment, which included such features as dual exhausts, heavy-duty shock absorbers, heavy-duty springs and a front stabilizer to maximize control in high-speed handling. Heavy-duty suspension had been available for several years, but had to be specially ordered. Now it was standard on the GTO. The 389 cubic-inch V8 came standard with a four-barrel carb and 335hp. An optional triple two-barrel carb version put out 360hp in 1965. The standard gearbox was a three-speed synchromesh with an optional four-speed with a Hurst linkage. The GTO was a full, factory-packaged hot-rod that sold for just under $3000 in 1966.

GTO handling, thanks to the heavy-duty suspension and stabilizer bar, got raves from American sports car enthusiast magazines that had paid little attention to previous Detroit pavement-rippers because of their crude handling. The GTO, like the costly Chrysler 300, was a fast V8 sedan that could do more than go in a straight line. The GTO had admirable road-holding for a sedan of its time and paved the way for future Detroit performance sedans that would combine brilliant acceleration with good handling.

With a tyre-smoking engine in an intermediate-size car with a glamorous, distinctive shape, the GTO was important in the development of the 'niche-market' car – cars carefully tailored to appeal to a small but precisely defined sector of the buying public. The niche for this car was the person who wanted a tough, fast car with a good-looking shape and a moderate price tag. The GTO was a market success beyond all expectation for such a performance-oriented package. Sales shot up from 32 000 in 1964 to 97 000 in 1966.

The GTO put Mustang in the shade as a performance car until Carroll Shelby worked his California hot-rodding magic on a special-edition Mustang called the GT-350. The GT-350 came about as a result of Ford president Lee Iacocca asking Shelby if he could make a racing car out of the Mustang. It was 1965 and the Cobra

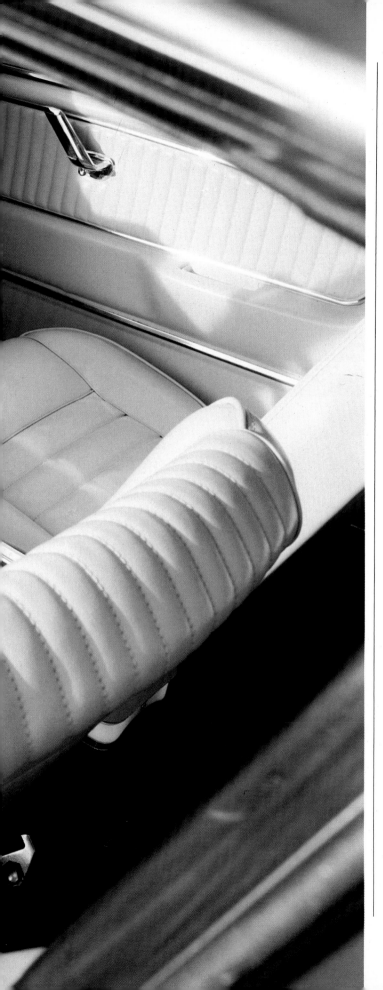

was winning; Iacocca wanted to see if the Mustang could win too. In the version Shelby cooked up, it could and did.

The GT-350 was like a GTO carried several steps further in the direction of all-out performance. It started out as a Mustang with a 271hp 289 cubic-inch V8 and a four-speed synchromesh gearbox. At the Shelby American works in Los Angeles, the Mustangs were converted into race cars or ferocious street cars. The conversion involved a thorough job of souping up the motor to produce 306hp. Suspension was beefed up, realigned and modified with traction control rods for better handling. The battery was moved to the trunk to improve weight distribution and the steel hood was replaced by a fibreglass hood to save weight.

In pursuit of lightness, the rear seats were removed, making clear the GT-350's seriousness of purpose. This was a performance car pure and simple. The racing version of the car was modified considerably beyond the specifications of the street cars, so much so

Below: 1966 GT-350 Mustang

The Mustang was available in a performance-only version produced by Carroll Shelby, the man behind the Cobra. Like a little brother to the mighty Cobra, the Shelby Mustang GT-350 was a ferocious, rough-riding road-runner which put all other functions secondary to all-out speed. The GT-350 was designed to win races. It did. It was intended to win championships. It did. The GT-350, not surprisingly, became an instant legend.

that it was totally restricted to the racetrack. The racing GT-350 was so effective it beat the Corvette Sting Ray in winning the US National Road-Racing Championship in 1966.

The street GT-350s gave a major boost to the Ford Mustang performance image, and the car inspired almost as pervasive a legend as its bigger brother the Cobra. The GT-350 had its own uniform, with a solid colour paint scheme decorated with two wide racing stripes down the front hood, over the roof and continuing over the rear deck. There was a trim stripe along the lower belt-line and the name GT-350. As in the GTO, the initials stood for *gran turismo*, an Italian

Left: 1965 Mustang Fastback

The popular GT option featured a three-spoke sport steering wheel and colour-keyed interior with pleated vinyl trim for a level of luxury at an unprecedented low price. Bucket seats were ordered on 97 per cent of all Mustangs sold, and 65 per cent had V8 engines.

expression that means 'grand touring' in English, and 'bitchin'' in Californian. The number 350 had no special meaning at all. It was just a number Shelby liked.

The GT-350 got high marks for performance in the auto-enthusiast press, but the car's shortcomings were noted. To achieve the breathtaking speed and near racetrack-level handling, ride comfort, noise level and tractability were seriously compromised. While the GTO offered high performance with all the comforts of a sedan, the GT-350 was a no-compromise, all-out performance car with comfort be damned. The GT-350's single-purpose nature limited sales to a trickle — fewer than 1500 a year — and fuelled the legend of one of the outstanding American performance cars.

The GT-350 was eventually a victim of its own publicity success. The prestige of the name was so important to the corporate image that Ford wanted the Shelby Mustang mass-produced, which meant moving it back to Detroit and out of Shelby's hands. The result was a watered-down image car for the mass market with a blunted performance edge and an eventual loss of identity.

But the excitement created by two-door American performance cars brought more new cars into being. In 1966, Plymouth brought out the two-door fastback Barracuda and Dodge produced the two-door fastback Charger. Pontiac brought out the two-door Firebird and Chevrolet produced the Camaro as a counter to the Mustang. A sporty, two-door mid-size Chevrolet,

the Camaro carried the Pontiac 'Coke-bottle' rear fender curve into a dominant contour for the whole rear of the car. With a long hood, a short, snubbed rear deck and tail, a low top and a wide track, the Camaro had a muscular grace that put it ahead of the pony car pack in style.

The Camaro was either a hardtop coupe or convertible; there was no utilitarian sedan version. Engine and trim options covered a wide spectrum. The wildest package was the Z28 in 1967, the performance-trim option that converted a standard Camaro into a high-performance American GT car, clearly aimed at the GT-350. Because a convertible is prone to chassis flex under high torque loads, the Z28 was available only in the coupe version, and with front disc brakes.

The Z28 package included a heavy-duty radiator with a temperature-controlled fan, special quick steering, dual exhaust, special wheels and heavy-duty suspension. There were white 'rallye stripes' on the hood and deck, like the GT-350, and the Z28 identification on the fenders. A road-racing version of the Z28 was developed, with factory support, to battle the Mustang in the popular Trans-Am Series. The street Z28, like a GT-350 with padding and seat cushions left in, was a performance car made for handling curves as well as straight lines and for stopping as well as accelerating. Though far more comfortable and tractable than the GT-350, the Z28 was a genuine performance car in the same vein as the Shelby Mustang.

1966 Dodge Charger
Chrysler's answer to the Mustang and the GTO was the Dodge Charger. Never as successful as either, the Charger created a legend of its own with its purposeful, sinister shape and one of the mightiest performance engines of all time. The Charger was one of several Chrysler-family cars that featured the fearsome hemi-head 426 cubic-inch V8. A Dodge hemi-Charger was an expensive car to buy and even more expensive to insure. It was not a particularly easy car to keep in proper tune. But when the pedal went down, a Dodge hemi-Charger turned into one of the fastest cars on earth.

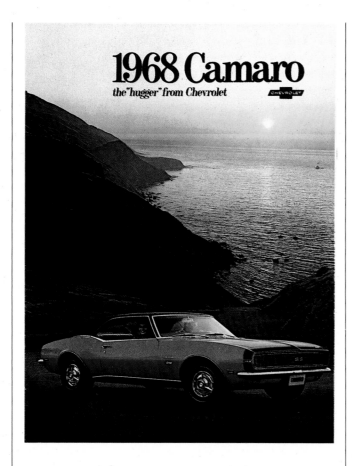

1968 Camaro
the "hugger" from Chevrolet

Far left: 1968 Chevrolet Camaro Z28
Left: 1968 Chevrolet Camaro
The Camaro was GM's main response to the Mustang, part of a wave of fifties' cars known as pony cars. The Camaro came in a wide variety of flavours and shapes, much like the Mustang.

Below: The Dodge Charger used by the villains in the thriller *Bullitt* remains a masterful image of the sinister automobile – a two-ton hunk of high-speed menace that meets its end in an apocalyptic crash.

wheels and a vinyl-covered top – one of the rare uses of that feature which did not look like an add-on decoration from a motel lounge. Engine options included both the 426 hemi-head and the 440 Magnum wedgehead. The 426 hemi was an evolutionary development of the 396 cubic-inch engine that gave Chrysler so many NASCAR wins in 1954 and 1955. It was the engine that powered the mighty Chrysler 300 letter series cars, and produced such prodigious power that it was the reigning engine in unlimited drag racing from the fifties onward.

The 426 hemi option gave the Charger a top speed of over 150 mph, which made it one of the fastest cars not just in the United States, but in the world. It had the looks to match the mystique of the mighty hemi. It looked as potent as it was. A black Charger driven by the villains in the thriller *Bullitt* starred in one of the all-time great movie car chases. Driven by professional assassins stalking the detective played by Steve McQueen, the Charger left a lasting impression as a vehicle of menace before exploding in a fiery, apocalyptic ending.

But the days of the supercars were numbered. They were slowed by 1967 Federal safety and emissions standards – soon to be followed by the Clean Air Act

The Camaro Z28 was a sophisticated alternative to the brute horsepower approach normally followed with Detroit performance cars. Instead of a massive engine, the Z28 used the high rpm capability of an extremely efficient small-block 302 cubic-inch V8 to deliver thrilling performance. For the driver willing to use the four-speed transmission to keep the revs up in the power band, and interested in negotiating curves as well as straight lines at speed, the Z28 was a milestone American performance car, even though sales were small. Chevy made other Camaros with bigger motors for drag racing enthusiasts.

The Dodge Charger did not follow the GT-350 and the Z28 in the direction of all-round high-performance. The Charger had the biggest, most powerful V8 on the market and, with a body change in 1968, the sleek hardtop had more style than any other muscle car on the road. The 1968 Charger had graceful fuselage styling with a tunnel-back rear window, and a 'Coke-bottle' curve for the mid-section and rear fender. The extended tail and sculpted nose gave it a more aerodynamic look than the Camaro or the Mustang. It was a blatant invitation to speed.

The Charger had a blacked-out grille, styled steel

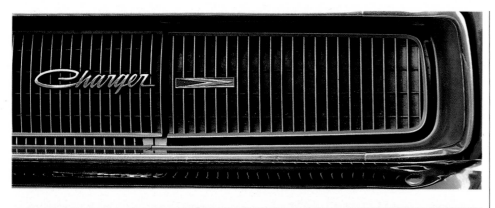

1968 Dodge Charger
and overleaf

A matte-black flush front grille covered the recessed headlights for a smooth, sleek look in front. Side safety lights were a new feature for 1968. The tail continued the matte-black application, handsomely setting off the distinctive twin taillights. A racing-type outside gas filler cap was mounted on the left fender. The Charger was a rare example of a harmonious design that blended all the popular styling cues of the time, uncluttered by excessive stripes or overdone trim.

of 1970 – which expressed mounting concern over the damage to the environment from exhaust pollutants. At the same time, auto-insurance rates caught up with performance and the cost of driving a supercar escalated. Though engines got bigger after 1968, absolute performance declined, and most of the supercars were to be tamed within a few years. But rather than produce different cars to satisfy evolving tastes, Detroit continued to try to make the same kinds of cars, adapting them to meet the new standards. It was not altogether faulty reasoning. Americans still had a powerful appetite for big, powerful, high-styled cars. The difference by the end of the sixties was that there were new market segments for small efficient cars, small glamour-image cars and small high-performance

1967 VW Beetle
While Detroit engines got bigger and cars got faster, the homely VW Beetle drew growing numbers of fans with its lack of style, lack of performance and reverse image. The VW became a counter-culture automotive badge of protest in the second half of the sixties.

cars. It was here that foreign manufacturers came into their own.

Detroit was not blind to the rising popularity of foreign sports cars, which had grown from cult status in the early fifties to widespread popularity by the early sixties, when MG, Triumph and Austin-Healey were the collegiate favourites and Porsche the car for snobs who wore driving gloves and listened to Mahler on FM radio. But a more important market factor was the Porsche's proletarian ancestor, the Volkswagen. A trickle of VW sales in the fifties had swelled to a flood in the sixties. This was puzzling. The success story of the American auto business of the fifties was adding so much luxury, power and style to low-price cars that the distinction between economy and luxury cars

Right: **1964 VW Beetle**
Below: **1967 VW Beetle**
Beetles were used for transportation, travel, communal living, loving, parking and partying. It was a long journey for the pre-World War II German People's Car to become the new symbol for anti-establishment American youth, but VW did it.

blurred. But the VW was selling without style, size, power or any hint of luxury. It had no image except what it was: a car designed for Hitler as a German counterpart to the Model T Ford — a people's car. What was the German people's car of the thirties doing in the American market in the sixties?

Much of the answer lay in changes in American society. While the pony cars and muscle cars and super-cars were still duking it out, a new cultural wave was rising with a consciousness that had no place for glamorous performance cars. The long-haired hippies, activists and counter-culturists who were changing the balance of power on the street and on the campus adopted the VW Beetle as a social protest vehicle as much as for transport. As the music of the Beatles, Jefferson Airplane, the Grateful Dead and the Who echoed from love-ins to mass rock concerts, the VW Beetle was everywhere. Beetles were parked at communes in Taos, at demonstrations in Berkeley, on the street in Ann Arbor and Cambridge, on the highway driving coast-to-coast. The VW was the vehicle of the sixties student protest movement, the Love Generation, and every longhair wearing beads, sandals, jeans, smocks and tie-dyed shirts.

But the spartan VW had already developed a significant following in middle-class America before getting adopted as a badge of counter-culture on wheels. A brilliant Madison Avenue advertising campaign had helped sell VWs to a rapidly growing number of Americans who thought Detroit cars were oversized, overstyled, overpowered and overpriced. The VW buyers were at the opposite end of the economic scale from the blue-collar workers the car had been designed for in Germany — an economy car that had succeeded at a time when the mere fact of automobile ownership was status in itself.

Shortly after World War II, steel magnate Henry J. Kaiser had tried to sell Americans the idea of a small, budget-priced economy car named after himself. The Henry J was low-cost transport without flair or frills, and it failed because flair and frills were what Americans wanted – which is why Chevrolets that mimicked Cadillacs sold so well, and why blue-collar Americans shunned the VW Beetle.

But by doing without ornamentation or style alto-gether, the VW introduced the minimalist style of function as form. And because VW buyers tended to be professionals or students, the Beetle gradually developed its own status. The VW Beetle was firmly established as a vehicle of choice for millions of Americans who preferred it to flashier, more powerful cars. And the field had expanded to include the Toyota Corona and Corolla as the first of the Japanese cars that would reshape the American car market a decade later. Datsun was part of the incoming Japanese tide, selling 2629 cars in 1962. In 1965 the sales were up to 12 600

Below and bottom right:
1964 VW Beetle
The VW was stark and functional inside, everything the American car was not. After a generation of bigness and betterness and moreness, the VW appealed to those who wanted less in a car.

Above: 1963 Porsche Carrera

Porsche was a designer label car, an elitist vehicle with the snob appeal of the Lacoste crocodile shirt. Small and understated by design, Porsche glamour came from the aura of superior quality and refined performance, qualities appreciated by the initiates and ignored by the unwashed masses. Porsche was a status symbol for those who enjoyed a car whose prestige value lay in what it was not.

cars and 5300 trucks and by 1969 total sales were 86 800. The sub-compact economy import was the shape of things to come.

Another shape was Porsche, which had developed a strong identity as a new kind of image car – a small car with a small engine that delivered exciting performance to the initiate, without risk of attracting the lower orders who preferred the rumbling smoke and fire of a big V8. Porsche was a designer-label car, an elitist's car, a snob-appeal car for the wearer of Lacoste crocodile shirts and top-sider shoes. It had the potent reverse-snob appeal of costing more and looking like less, guaranteeing that those who drove one were secure in their social status. Previous status cars were either bigger, flashier or faster than other cars – or all three. Automotive status had been a factor of show and clout. With the Porsche of the early sixties, it took on another dimension to include the appeal of the car noticed and appreciated only by those who knew – which meant the educated elite.

Cadillac was still the top status car for most Americans, but the encroachment of German, Italian and English cars was growing. The presence of Mercedes-Benz and BMW was already becoming a factor in the automotive scene that had not yet registered its proper impact in Detroit. It soon would.

The sixties had reached a peak of mellow sharing and celebration of love as the hopeful dawning of a New Age at Woodstock in the summer of 1969. A year later a rock festival featuring the Rolling Stones at Altamont in northern California turned violent. The heroes of the age of Aquarius died – Janis Joplin, Jimi Hendrix, Jim Morrison – and a ghoul named Charles Manson spread terror and murder through southern California in the name of demented love, ending the sixties with a scream.

On the last album Janis Joplin recorded before she died was a prophecy of Detroit's automotive decline: *Lord, won't you buy me a Mercedes-Benz.*

THE EARLY SEVENTIES

The Cadillac Eldorado
as the Colossus of Roads and the
crumbling of an empire

At the beginning of the seventies, America's long-running romance with the big car and V8 performance clashed with environmental consciousness and ecology. Federal noise and emissions law standards led to the largest engines ever produced to maintain performance. Cadillac produced a 500 cubic-inch V8 for the Eldorado in the last gasp of American supremacy. The Arab oil embargo and fuel price inflation sliced off the American dream at the knees. Fuel efficient, economy imports started a rising tide of demand for change. Porsche deposed Corvette as the king of the street and the Datsun 240Z redefined the low-priced sports car. Japanese and German imports chipped away at Detroit's ownership of the home auto market.

CADILLAC rode out the turmoil of the Watergate scandal, demonstrations against the bombing of Cambodia and the national body blow of the Arab oil embargo as a luxury car should: with an increasingly long wheelbase, more power and a soft ride that insulated driver and passengers from any discomfort.

Through the fifties and sixties, low-priced American cars had grown larger and more luxurious, narrowing the gap in size, silhouette and luxury level between Chevy and Cadillac, Ford and Lincoln, Dodge and Chrysler. But there was no question that in the early seventies, Cadillac was still the wish-fulfilment car for most Americans. Cadillac's market share had increased almost every year since 1950, and in 1973 sales passed the 300 000 mark for an all-time record. While Cadillac was gaining ground, doubling its sales in ten years, other American cars, including Chevrolet, stood still. Chevrolet sales for 1973 were only 1 per cent higher than in 1961.

Cadillac, of course, was bigger than ever in 1970. So were all the other Detroit cars. But Cadillac, as befits the leading American luxury car, had the biggest engine and the most power of any of the luxury three, with a 472 cubic-inch V8 rated at 375hp, compared to the 365hp Lincoln 460 V8 and 375hp from the Chrysler 440 V8. All three big American cars dwarfed European models like Rolls-Royce, which made do with 380 cubic inches, and Mercedes-Benz, which managed to cope with a meagre 278.

But a 472 cubic-inch V8 was only enough for the standard Cadillac models. In 1970, the ultra-luxury Eldorado got a V8 that displaced 500 cubic inches – one of the largest auto engines of all time – and put out a claimed 400hp. Weighing a massive 4600 pounds, the Eldorado was no match at speed for the 427 Corvette or the hottest muscle cars, but its power was not to be trifled with.

The Eldorado of 1970 was a middle-aged version of the Thunderbird – a two-door hardtop coupe for rich people who dreamed young. The Eldorado sold for roughly $9000 with the $2000 vinyl padded roof, twice the price of a fully loaded Chevrolet Impala custom coupe. But there was value for dollars even apart from the name, image and luxury trim. Cadillac still maintained the leadership in technology that had always been part of its claim to supremacy. Besides

Left: **1974 Cadillac**
Right: **1969 Cadillac Eldorado**
When the world was scored by violent upheaval and the American economy had become a shambles, Cadillac lengthened its wheelbase for a softer ride and enlarged its engine for more power. While the 472 cubic-inch Cadillac V8 was a monster in the automotive world, it was not deemed enough for the ultra-luxury Eldorado. For 1970, Cadillac upped the displacement of the two-door Eldorado sports coupe to a whopping 500 cubic inches, one of the largest engines ever installed in an automobile. The Eldorado was a statement in indulgence, with lists of extra luxury options adding thousands of dollars to an already highly priced car.

having the biggest engine, the Eldorado shared with the Oldsmobile Toronado the distinction of being America's only front-wheel-drive cars, adding the bonus of an advanced drive-train to sheer brute power.

While compact cars were clearly the new wave, big cars continued getting bigger. Cadillac grew from 228 inches overall in 1970 to 234 inches in 1974, keeping an imperial edge over Chevrolet which went from 216 to 223 inches in the same years. Luxury-car price-per-pound weight had gone up only a little since the fifties, with Cadillac selling for $1.48 per pound in 1970, compared to $1.00 per pound for Chevrolet. By 1974, Cadillac was up to $1.78 per pound and Chevrolet had risen to $1.10 per pound.

With the 1971 introduction of the sub-compact four-cylinder Vega to replace the failed Corvair, Chevrolet had ten separate model lines. The Vega was an immediate market success with 350 000 first-year sales, but the bulk of Chevrolet sales volume was larger cars. Chevrolet's biggest V8 had increased from 427 cubic inches to 454 cubic inches, with the Corvette 454 rated at 460hp, the highest power rating of any production car engine in history.

1974 Cadillac Eldorado
In the early 1970s, Cadillac was at its peak of success in post-war America, the car more people aspired to than any other. Hedonism and excess ruled the interior of the Eldorado. The curved dashboard with digital clock were new for 1974; tilt dash telescope steering wheel, cruise control, climate control and six-way power seats were optional. With front-wheel drive and front disc brakes, the Eldorado boasted advanced engineering features that appeared to justify its expense and position of status leadership.

The American love of big engines was not without its cost, however, even for the wealthy. Emission standards were to tighten in the seventies and the challenge of meeting them without losing horsepower and performance would eventually require new technology – although Cadillac dealt with the first-stage controls by increasing engine size from 429 to 472 cubic inches for a power gain of 35hp. The Arab oil embargo, the long lines at gas stations and the quadrupling of prices in 1974 temporarily traumatized the nation and hit the domestic auto industry hard. Yet, though sales of full-size American cars were affected most, Cadillac sales suffered least of all. A popular option for 1974 was an interior package called the Fleetwood Brougham Talisman (including leather upholstery) which cost $2450 extra – more than the full price of a new Vega compact. While Cadillac's sales total was below its 1973 record, the decrease was much smaller than the industry average and Cadillac actually increased its market share in a steady growth pattern that continued throughout the seventies.

It was a strange time. The spirit of the sixties was still alive but the confident Aquarian Age glow of peace

and love had faded with the multiple shocks of a public killing at a California Rolling Stones concert, the horror of the Charles Manson cult murders, and the sudden deaths of Janis Joplin, Jim Morrison and Jimi Hendrix. Robert Kennedy, the political hope for so many children of the sixties, had gone down to an assassin's bullets, along with Martin Luther King, and the vengeful spirit of Richard Nixon ruled in Washington.

Long hair had become fashion instead of an ID badge of the counter-culture. Underground music had gone overground along with FM radio and rock had become the American beat. Though the Beach Boys and even the Beatles had celebrated cars and driving in

The darker side of the automobile in America surfaced in movies in the late sixties. The deadly fireballs that ended the pursuits in *Bullitt* and *Vanishing Point* reflected the annual carnage on the highways and the spasms of political and pop-cultural life that ended the sixties on a note of pain.

the sixties, there was a darker vision in movies. Films featured a chilling level of violence on wheels. After the bloody finale of *Bonnie and Clyde* came the murderous fireball that finished the car chase in *Bullitt*, the bloody executions at the end of *Easy Rider*, the explosive crash at the climax of the existential car chase of *Vanishing Point*.

Violence in film, of course, was inevitable in a country with a generation at war. It was also the underside of the American love affair with the auto, the twentieth-century convenience that killed almost as many people every year as the total number of American deaths in Vietnam. The grim numbers of the

1969 Boss 302 Mustang
and overleaf
Produced with the SCCA's Trans-Am racing series in mind, Ford's Boss Mustang offered extraordinary performance features for a production street car. The engine was practically hand-built to racing tolerances, with forged pistons, an aluminium manifold, a forged crankshaft and four-bolt main bearings. The Boss Mustangs, like the Camaro Z28 and the Plymouth 'Cuda, offered a combination of exciting performance with refined road-holding that was unusually advanced for a production sedan.

highway fatality roll, which claimed over 40 000 lives annually, did not change substantially from one year to the next. Nor did they seem to have any impact on the national consciousness. Violence and sudden death had always been prominent in American films, just as violence and sudden death had been major forces in American history. An awareness that fast cars and violent death might be linked had no more deterrent effect on sales than the statistical links between cigarette smoking and cancer, or alcohol and homicide. Cars were still the most important possession for most non-homeowners and the second most important possession for those who did own their homes.

A new kind of car had grown up with the post-war generation. In the five years since *Mustang Sally* hit the pop charts, the Mustang had gone downhill. Added inches and pounds blunted the fine edge of style and performance that made the Mustang special, and Mustang lost the pony car performance edge to the hot Camaro Z28. In 1969 Ford countered the Z28 with the Boss 302 Mustang and supported a factory team in a new sports car racing division for small American sedans called the Trans-American Cup series. Ford, like Chevrolet and Chrysler, had been active in stock-car racing and drag racing since the early fifties. But Trans-Am racing was different. The Trans-Am series,

sanctioned by the Sports Car Club of America (SCCA), pitted America's small performance cars against each other on national road racecourses in contests watched by hundreds of thousands. The epic battles between Ford and Chevrolet in pursuit of the championship heightened interest in both cars, and the win by Parnelli Jones in the 1970 championship gave the Boss Mustang image a tremendous boost.

Like the Z28, the street-model Boss 302 was a snarling tyre-smoker that lived up to its name, which was slang for 'hip', 'cool' or 'groovy'. With new 'sportsroof' fastback lines the 1969-70 Mustang was an improvement on the original styling and far better looking than the Mustangs to follow. Though it had a clean shape, the Boss 302 was as subtle as a fire engine. The garish side-stripes, the blacked-out hood and grille and the bordello-style venetian-slat louvered exterior rear-window shade were standard Boss 302 items, along with the paint colours, which included Grabber Orange, Grabber Green and Grabber Blue for the customer who wanted something louder than the standard Bright Yellow, Acapulco Blue, Calypso Coral and Wimbledon White.

The Boss 302 was a borderline cartoon-car, which is what it would have been without the performance options list. The special features included low-profile

1969 Boss 302 Mustang
Along with the high-compliance shocks and heavy-duty suspension, the package included special custom performance wheels and tyres. The Boss Mustang was overstyled then and looks overstyled now. The gimmicky trim was part of the effort to produce a car that said style and performance anywhere you looked.

Above: **1969 Boss 429 Mustang**
Left: **1969 Ford Mustang GT-500**
The Boss 429 was an all-out drag racer, a single-purpose street fighting vehicle dedicated to straight-line performance and nothing else. The Shelby GT-500 was proof that Ford, like all American auto companies, was never above ruining a good thing by trying to make it bigger and better. The Shelby GT-350 lost its sharply defined character when enlarged to the GT-500, and became just another mass-produced American car that promised more than it delivered. The degeneration of the Shelby Mustang was a familiar story in post-war American auto-making – another special car falling victim to its own success.

Goodyear F60 × 15 fibreglass-belted wide oval tyres on special 15 in × 7 in rims, quick-ratio steering and a heavy-duty four-speed transmission with a Hurst shift handle. Handling was covered with heavy-duty springs and front shocks, front and rear anti-sway bars and special staggered rear shocks to improve traction under full-power applications. The handling package worked. Bigger-engined Mustangs could go faster in a straight line, but none could start, stop and take curves or bumpy roads better than a Boss 302.

The engine was an extraordinary package for a street machine – an aluminium high-rise manifold, heavy-duty connecting rods, forged pistons and a forged steel crankshaft with four-bolt main bearings – expensive items normally found only in custom-built motors. The power output claimed from all this was 290hp at 5800 rpm, the same rating Chevrolet gave the Z28. The figures for both cars were conservative, reversing a long-standing practice of overstating horsepower. This was not a belated attack of corporate truth in packaging, but an effort to spare buyers the steep liability insurance premiums imposed on high horsepower machines.

Horsepower and performance had always been sensitive issues with the government and the public. They became more sensitive in the early seventies.

While enthusiasts, especially teenage males, loved speed and believed more power was better, a far greater number of people shared a concern voiced by congress that saw fast cars as a possible threat to public health. The blatant street-racing packages coming out of Detroit were causing rumbles in Washington and negative comments in the press. After several years of open factory participation in auto racing, Henry Ford II declared an end to company-supported racing after the 1970 season. The Ford engine option sheet for 1971 still listed ten different V8s in varying stages of tune and horsepower from 210hp up to 375hp. But the Trans-Am series withered and faded without

1970 Plymouth AAR 'Cuda 340

The 'Cuda was custom tailored for the dedicated street speed freak. Its package included special wheels and tyres, a Hurst shifter, racing-car type hood latches, anti-glare black-out paint on the hood with black accent stripes on the body to announce its streetfighting mission.

factory support, and the Boss 302 was discontinued. There was new styling for 1971 and a third-generation Mustang with modern but unattractive lines which suffered weak sales in 1971 and dropped even further for 1972.

The good looks of the second-generation Mustang were equalled and perhaps outdone by the 1970 Plymouth Barracuda, the third generation of a car that first appeared in 1965 as a fastback Valiant with styling an apparent afterthought. The second-generation Barracuda in 1968 had much-improved styling and the all-new shape for 1970 was even better. The long hood, deep-raked windshield, rounded sides and short

125

snub-tail gave the Barracuda an image of speed and power with graceful, elegant lines that somehow looked classic and modern at the same time.

The AAR 'Cuda 340 was named for Dan Gurney's All-American Racers, the team that campaigned it for Plymouth in the 1970 Trans-Am series. Though it was unable to beat Ford and Chevy on the track, the new 'Cuda succeeded on the street with 1970 sales up almost 50 per cent over 1969. The 335hp AAR 'Cuda 340 was a reasonably balanced package that included heavy-duty suspension, white-letter tyres on wide rims, and special exterior trim to announce its street-fighting mission. The trim included a hood blacked out against glare in racing-car fashion, broken black accent stripes along the body, and wire hood-pin locks like racing car hood latches.

The AAR 'Cuda also offered a four-speed synchro-mesh gearbox with a Hurst shifter available instead of the factory shift lever. The option of a shift lever mechanism made by an after-market supplier instead of the factory equipment shows how far the influence of hot-rodding extended in Detroit. The Hurst shifter was a massive chromed steel stem that made the factory gearshift lever seem puny and inadequate. Chrysler could have manufactured a close replica, but it would have lacked the appeal of the Hurst name.

George Hurst was the genius behind the marketing of this beefier shift lever that made quick gear changes easier and had a look and feel coveted by every young

1970 Plymouth AAR 'Cuda 340

The Plymouth AAR 'Cuda was designed to compete in the Trans-Am sports car racing series dominated by Ford's Boss Mustang and the Camaro Z28. To meet Trans-Am racing engine size limits, the AAR 'Cuda was powered by the 340 cubic-inch V8, the junior of Chrysler's performance engines. The AAR 'Cuda 340 was fine-tuned for maximum power output at high rpm, with a close-ratio four-speed gearbox. Though the 'Cuda was as handsome a styling package as any car of the time, the racing effort could not match Ford and Chevrolet and the 'Cuda never succeeded on the track.

hot-rodder in the country. The Hurst shifter followed a convoluted evolutionary trail to arrive as a factory option in Detroit muscle cars of the late sixties and early seventies. It dated back to the late thirties, when gearshift levers had been moved from the floor to the steering column as a luxury, putting the lever closer to hand. In the fifties the convenience of automatic transmissions phased out manual shifting except for performance cars, whose drivers did not care about convenience. Synchromesh gearboxes were developed to accommodate performance fans, and four-speed transmissions became a high-status item. Furthermore, the shift lever was then moved back from the steering column down to the floor again for more direct, positive shifting.

Because the passenger compartment was spatially different in the late fifties from that of the thirties when floor shifts were standard, the seat interfered with the shift lever in drag racing speed-shifts. The Hurst shifter solved the space problem with a boomerang curve, made of heavy forged steel for durability. Instead of an ordinary knob, there was an angled pistol grip contoured to fit the hand perfectly. Because the Hurst shift linkage improved fast gear changing it became standard equipment for professional drag racers. That made every amateur drag racer and would-be drag racer want one.

To enhance the image, Hurst appointed a spectacularly curved Georgia beauty-contest winner named

Linda Vaughan as Miss Hurst Golden Shifter. Linda Vaughan linked the Hurst name with success, sex and glamour by giving victory kisses to winners at drag racing and stock-car racing championships through the sixties and seventies. The Hurst shifter became just as popular with stock-car racers and their fans as it was in drag racing and the name Hurst came to be synonymous with performance. It was an example of a product's popularity promoting itself and its own name becoming a selling point.

For Detroit to equip performance cars with accessories

1967 Corvette Stingray 427 and overleaf
A fire-breather for the die-hard thrill-seeker, the 427 Corvette was overkill in a time of ultra-cars. Built for full-force, racetrack acceleration and mind-warp top speed, it became an instant legend.

which were usually added on by hot-rodders completed a circle that had begun long before. In the early fifties, hot-rodders customized their cars with style tricks and parts that did not come from the factory. In the sixties Detroit was copying hot-rodders and by 1970 the performance cars came already customized for looks and performance.

Youth-market performance cars were hot in Detroit. Pontiac had created the GTO as a budget performance car in 1964 and followed it with the down-sized, sporty two-door Firebird, the Pontiac version of the

Camaro. In 1970 Pontiac introduced the Firebird Trans-Am, named for the racing series. Ironically, the Pontiac Trans-Am never made a dent in the series it was named for, but went on to sales success that outshone the Camaro Z28, winner of the 1968 and 1969 Trans-Am championships.

The Firebird Trans-Am started out as a competition-oriented car, but with the demise of the racing series Pontiac refocused the Trans-Am from bona fide road-racer to performance-image car. In that role, the Trans-Am outsold the Z28 by a wide margin. The secret of the Trans-Am's success on the street was styling overstatement. It had worked before, when flamboyance and cosmetic excess sold cars in the late fifties. It worked again in the late seventies with the visual overkill of the wide fender flares, bulging hood scoop and a huge 'screaming chicken' hood decal that should have embarrassed everyone but instead probably sold cars. Though all pretence of being a finely honed road-race machine had been abandoned, the Trans-Am kept muscle car performance alive through the Arab oil embargo and the crisis that followed, offering the formidable HO Super Duty 455 V8 in 1974 when others had given up. But times were changing fast.

The 1970 Clean Air Act imposed a tightening web of controls on automobile engines to relieve the smog pollution that putrefied air in Los Angeles and other cities. Engine and exhaust noise were restricted, safety

1979 Pontiac Firebird Trans-Am

The Firebird Trans-Am was created to capitalize on the youth market for specialized performance cars. The Trans-Am took its name directly from the racing series which had spawned the other New Age muscle cars. But the Trans-Am hardly scored a point on the track in a racing effort that was a slow second to Chevrolet. The Trans-Am didn't need racetrack success. Its looks, image and street performance were enough to make it a hit. What buyers wanted, it seemed, was not the racetrack performance of the Z28 and the 'Cuda, but the drag-strip manners of the big-engined Trans-Am. The styling was overdone and corny. It should have embarrassed everyone, but instead it sold cars.

standards required heavier bumpers and new cars had to burn unleaded gasoline. Then the gas shortage following the Arab oil embargo triggered Federal fuel-economy standards that would eventually halt the long period of growth in size and performance. The combined impact of emissions and mileage regulations took the heart out of most American performance-car engines, including the Corvette. Horsepower of the 454 cubic-inch Chevy V8 fell off sharply in 1973 and dropped again in 1974. In 1975 the 454 engine was discontinued and Corvette was relegated to secondary status among world-class performance cars. The decline of the Corvette coincided with the rise of German and Japanese cars as a force on the American performance-car market, reflecting a shift in the global balance of power that would fundamentally alter the American automobile business.

Detroit's initial response to the schedule of emissions and mileage standards was to complain that they were beyond the reach of technology. But while Detroit executives lobbied in Washington for relaxation of the new regulations, Volvo and Honda met the standards with cars that suffered neither price, nor performance, nor fuel-economy penalties. The pendulum had begun to swing away from America as the seat of world power. It was losing market share to foreign companies that had never before been taken seriously as competition. VW sales had steadily risen from the fifties and now cut deeply into American compact-car sales.

Japanese compacts further eroded Detroit's small-car position, and the doubling of gasoline prices inevitably hastened the process by giving fuel-efficient compacts a market priority they had never had in the United States before.

Though GM and Ford had strong sales with the compact Chevy Vega and the Ford Pinto, the Japanese compacts offered the style and performance the domestic compacts lacked. In the early seventies Volkswagen, Honda, Toyota and Datsun packaged high fuel economy with style and a sense of quality that made their cars attractive beyond mere efficiency. And while their high-mileage compacts were catching on, Japanese auto-makers developed fuel-efficient performance engines to sell in an even wider market.

In 1970 Datsun introduced the 240Z as a new definition of the popular-priced sports car for the American market. A smooth-lined fastback coupe with a silhouette suggestive of a scaled-down Ferrari Daytona, the 240Z was an immediate success. In one

1971 Datsun 240Z
Part of a wave of small-engined imports that would change the face of automobiles in America, the Datsun 240Z was a sports car that arrived just as the popular British sports cars were in their death throes. Datsun's new sports car offered a better engine, transmission, styling and reliability than the British cars had. An instant hit, in one model generation the 240Z redefined the sports car in America.

market cycle, the $3995 Datsun 240Z effectively put the ailing MG, Triumph and Austin-Healey to sleep by shelving the open-air, rough-riding, under-powered roadster concept in favour of a modern, comfortable, weatherproof car that combined style, performance and reliability with a low price. While the British cars struggled with out-of-date engineering, the 240Z was a new car for the seventies. Rather than an over-burdened mini-sedan four-cylinder motor like MG and Sprite, the 240Z had an overhead-cam six-cylinder engine like a small Jaguar. It also had a five-speed synchromesh gearbox, independent suspension and disc brakes. More important, it was rattle-free and airtight for reliable, smooth travel. The 240Z offered sports performance without inconvenience or the sacrifice of comfort. That and an incredibly low price made it a runaway success in the United States.

The 240Z was a fresh new entry in the US sports car market when the Corvette image was moving away from serious performance. The percentage of

Corvettes ordered with four-speed manual transmission shifted from a 70 per cent majority in 1970 to a 33 per cent minority in 1974. Over the same period the car gained 400 pounds and lost over 100hp, which seriously weakened performance. But sales increased with the image and performance shift from hard to soft, attracting an older, more conservative buyer who did not care that Corvette lacked the power and speed to challenge Ferrari, Lamborghini and Porsche. It had the image, and that's what counted.

As a budget sports car the 240Z was no match for Corvette in acceleration. That territory had been staked and claimed by the new up-market performance force on American roads: Porsche. At $8000, the 1971 Porsche 911 was priced a notch above Cadillac and a notch-and-a-half above a loaded Corvette. Though the hyper-exotic 12-cylinder Ferrari Boxer and Lamborghini Countach were faster, at $40 000 and over they were priced out of the real world for most people, while Porsche was merely expensive. Porsche

Above: **1955 Porsche 550 Spyder**
Right: **1955 Porsche 356A Speedster**
Famed as the car James Dean died in, the Porsche became as much a thread of Californian pop culture as surfing. Though the Dean death car was the racing Spyder pictured, the car he drove on the street was the Speedster. Steve McQueen and Paul Newman also drove Porsche Speedsters, a special light weight version of the roadster that was stripped of all non-essential conveniences to be sold at an attractively low price for enthusiast use. An immediate hit when new, the Speedster is considered a classic today.

had always been costly for its size, the $4000 price tag of the small four-cylinder 356 coupe running at an exorbitant $2.15 per pound in 1961. But now it was actually more expensive than Cadillac, and the price worked out to $3.80 per pound. The extreme cost was new for Porsche, as was the extreme performance and the image that came with it.

It was the four-cylinder 356, a lineal descendant of the VW Beetle, that had woven the Porsche name into the fabric of the fifties and sixties. With the 356 Porsche, the small German company built a reputation for engineering and driving refinement when Porsche was beating bigger cars in world championship sports-car racing. It became a symbol of good living in southern California, where cars are the way of life and Porsches are almost religion. In 1956, the legendary 356 Speedster was the car to have. At one time or another James Dean, Paul Newman and Steve McQueen were all Speedster owners and it was still a car to have in California twenty years later.

1955 Porsche 356
From its arrival on the US sports car scene in the mid fifties, snob appeal was part of the Porsche image. It was expensive for its size, power and modest performance. British sports cars offered more bang for the buck but lacked the Porsche cachet of being an aesthete's car.

Porsche grew with the expanding American sports car consciousness in the sixties in which *Car & Driver* and *Road & Track* magazines played major roles. Those two incisive, well-written monthlies presented sports cars not only as superior engineering and better handling but as symbols of a better life. Sports cars were for the cultivated taste of those who knew. Even then high price was part of the prestige image that made Porsche a snob's car, a car for the sporting esthete who appreciated quality. Like all successful images, the Porsche image fed and fostered itself. With its smooth, functional, undecorated shape and un-glamorous engine, the car was a symbol of the Bauhaus

Left: **1955 Porsche 356A Speedster**
Below: **1973 Porsche 911E**
The smooth, rounded shape of the small-engined 356 Speedster embodied the Bauhaus credo of 'less is more' by providing refined understatement in design and performance. In 1965, the modest, small-engined car gave way to the sleek, svelte, high-powered 911. An all-new car with an overhead-cam six-cylinder alloy engine instead of the VW-derived four in the 356, the 911 had the power to challenge Corvette on its own terms.

'form follows function' doctrine. To the believer, Porsche represented the truth of the credo 'less is more'.

That changed in 1965 when Porsche retired the faithful four-cylinder 356 and introduced the powerful, sleek and elegant six-cylinder, overhead-cam 911. Equal in acceleration and top speed to the Camaro Z28 and the 300hp Corvette 327, with the new 911 Porsche had been reborn. From an agile lightweight that relied on refined handling and driver skill to challenge a Corvette on a winding road, the 911 became a car that could pick a street fight when and where it chose.

The 911 engine was enlarged twice to increase horsepower after 1967, and in 1973 the 180 cubic-inch 911S was faster than the Corvette 454, the biggest and baddest Corvette left. Porsche achieved its superior performance with a thousand pound weight advantage over the Corvette, and with overhead-camshaft engine technology that produced far more horsepower per cubic inch than the overhead-valve Chevy V8. In 1974, Porsche increased engine size again to hold performance against the next stage of emission regulations as Corvette got slower. Porsche had gone from less is more to more is more, and to complement the tyre-smoking, 148 mph performance, the 911 got flared fenders, magnesium wheels and tinted glass in a high-priced Stuttgart version of the Detroit muscle-car-trim syndrome without the silly decals. In 1974 and 1975 Porsche put script decals along the lower border of the Carreras, perhaps to rub in the fact that Porsche was the new king of the mountain.

The loss of Corvette's street-king image to Porsche did not show up as a decline in Corvette sales. Porsche sold barely a tenth as many 911s in the United States as Chevrolet sold Corvettes in a year, and Corvette sales seemed to follow their own undulations. But Porsche, which was rapidly remaking international road racing in its own image, was undeniably an important new player on the American street-performance scene. After first trouncing Corvette on the track, Porsche walloped Ferrari so badly that Ferrari pulled out and left sports-car racing to the 200 mph blitzkriegers from Stuttgart. By 1975, the American muscle car had been pronounced officially, if prematurely, extinct, Corvette was living off its image, and Porsche was becoming a new definition of American status on wheels. The 911 was such a hit in California that PORSCHE became that state's most-requested vanity-plate licence in the seventies.

While Porsche was staking a German claim to the American performance crown, Mercedes-Benz was gaining on Cadillac as a luxury status car. Cadillac was still the prestige machine for the millions of Americans who wanted a luxury liner with a huge engine, no matter what gasoline cost. But the nature of status and prestige decree that upper levels exist which are unknown or unnoticed by those below. With Cadillac marked as the prestige car for the masses, and with so many on the road, the discriminating sought something more exclusive. Lincoln and Chrysler had fallen out of contention as serious status cars, so it had to be a foreign car. Mercedes was it.

During the sixties Mercedes-Benz had developed a US image much as Porsche did, only more quietly, remaining a low-profile car in America until the arrival of the V8 450 series in 1973. Both the luxury sports two-seater 450SL and the luxury 450SE sedan seemed tailored for the US market. Both cars were everything Cadillac was not, except expensive, and in that they were more so. The Mercedes-Benz 450s lacked Cadillac's size, flamboyant styling and overstated decor.

1974 Porsche 911 Carrera
While Detroit was in the doldrums because of new Federal emission regulations which were stifling power, Porsche responded to the 1973 standards with a bigger engine for more horsepower than the year before. The 911 line-up, in three ascending stages of high performance, was powerful enough to whip almost any American production car in a straight line. On a winding road, a Porsche 911 was near invincible.

Instead, the Mercedes appealed to the sophisticate — or at least it started out that way.

Mercedes had much to offer the American prestige car-buyer. Besides the appeal of high price, there was an elegant tradition of impeccable design and the mystique of the world championship Mercedes race cars. But until the seventies, Mercedes styling had been pale to the American eye and the performance tame by comparison with American cars. Then the V8-powered 450s arrived with satisfying performance, distinctive, elegant shapes and a sense of high style completely absent in Cadillac. Mercedes, like Porsche, represented quality and status to those who knew. Those who did not saw only a smallish, square-cornered car with a massive price-tag and no opera moulding, brougham inserts or special brushed-steel exterior trim. The 450SE styling had a strong rectangular contour with a lowered belt-line that carried the rearward curve of the front bumper all the way to the rear bumper, blending traditional Mercedes authority with a new glamour and luxury.

With slightly over half the engine displacement of Cadillac, the 276 cubic-inch Mercedes V8 delivered comparable acceleration with far better over-the-road performance. Mercedes-Benz's high speed handling and road-holding were equal to that of a fine sports car and vastly outclassed Cadillac. In ordinary driving, the 450SL had the appeal of a luxury German Thunderbird, a sporty car that was not really a sports car but had the young, romantic sports-car image.

Of course, the $12 000 price put the 450SL beyond the reach of all but the wealthiest youths. It was almost three times the price of a Corvette, which made it three times as desirable to the new type of buyer emerging in the seventies. Mercedes-Benz took a fast hold on the American market, outselling Porsche by as large a margin as Cadillac outsold Corvette. By the end of the decade, Mercedes was a new synonym for status in many parts of the country.

While German prestige cars encroached on Detroit from above, Datsun and Honda were moving in from below. As early as 1973, Honda had met the emissions and mileage standards proposed by the Environmental Protection Agency for 1975 with a motor called the compound vortex controlled combustion (CVCC) or Civic for short. Previous export Hondas had been too small for the US market, but the Civic was just big enough, and it was introduced in 1975 to immediate success on both coasts. The Civic provided reasonably peppy performance from 71 cubic inches, and Honda

1975 Mercedes-Benz 450 SLC

During the 1960s, Mercedes-Benz was a low-profile, high-priced foreign luxury car rarely seen on American roads. The styling of the V8-powered 450 series brought Mercedes into the foremost styling wave of the 1970s: a distinctive, elegant shape with a strong rectangular contour and a low belt-line that blended traditional Mercedes authority with a new glamour and luxury. The sporty SL series two-seaters were in the tradition of the classic 1955–7 American T-Bird: sporty without being sports cars, romantic without being threatening. The SLC was a longer wheelbase coupe version of the popular 450 SL, which became the chic prestige image car of the seventies. Mercedes-Benz became such a prized status symbol that its sales were unhampered by the fact that the price tripled within the decade, due to fluctuations between the Deutsche Mark and dollar.

Left: 1964 VW Beetle
The VW Beetle evolved from a sixties cult anti-status car to a mainstream success in the early 1970s, in spite of its archaic technology. The Beetle's design was minimalist style, a style that evolved from anti-style hip to counter-culture chic, which became mainstream modern. Of course, the VW style really was no style at all. Instead, it was a pure expression of the German design ideal 'form follows function'.

Above: 1973 Honda Civic
The success of the Beetle made way for the Japanese conquest of the American auto market. Honda led the wave with the Civic, another exercise in minimalist design which featured front-wheel-drive engineering and technology that was as up to date as VW was old-fashioned.

quickly became part of the American landscape. The Honda had little style to sell, but it was half the price of a full-size domestic car, and a growing number of Americans saw the Honda CVCC as a car to drive out of preference, not financial need.

Datsun was way ahead of Honda in the US market in 1973, with the B-510 sub-compact sedan already a strong seller before the introduction of the 240Z. Unlike the Honda Civic, which appealed mainly as a car for agreeable and extremely economical transport, the Datsun B-510 had a following as an economy-compact sports sedan. It was styled like a miniature American sedan instead of a Japanese compact, which somehow was just right. Datsun sold over 250 000 B-510s in the United States in 1972, and was on the way to becoming a mini-Model A Ford of the seventies.

While the B-510 started from too small a market base to approach any of the Model A sales records, it had the brisk response of the 1931 Ford along with pleasing lines and low price. Like the Model A, it was

simple to work on, which invited engine and body modifications for performance and styling. The B-510 was a highly successful racer in the SCCA small sedan series, earning it a performance image. After-market sources manufactured dress-up kits with fender flares, spoilers and air dams to outfit the B-510 as a mini-racer.

The B-510 became a vehicle of teen car clubs, for racing on the street and in the Hollywood hills. It was turned into a low-buck sports machine by young Californians who customized it, souped it up and drove it as an ID badge like the custom Chevys and Fords of the early fifties. In its way, this modest auto became a dream car of its time.

THE LATE SEVENTIES

The dream changes as
America awakens to world reality

After three decades of continuous improvement, the full-size American V8 seemed destined for extinction like the dinosaur. Detroit gave up to emissions and economy regulations and gave the performance lead to foreign auto-makers, who adapted faster and better to the new regulations. The Japanese and the Europeans produced economy in a sporty, compact contemporary package that redefined the American image. As Corvette fell further behind in styling and performance, Porsche became the new performance status car along with the Ferrari V8. The pick-up truck showed surprising popularity as an all-round transportation vehicle in a highway throwback to the American frontier.

WHEN Cadillac finished the last of the 1976 Eldorado convertibles, by then the only convertible still in production, it seemed like the end of an era. It was the beginning of Jimmy Carter's one term as President, and the convertible was a victim of changing taste and shrinking demand.

Convertibles had always been the American dream on wheels, the epitome of glamour. They made ordinary people feel like movie stars. And good-looking cars always looked better as convertibles, especially the long, low, wide American cars of the fifties and sixties. Celebrities in parades waved to crowds and cameras on Fifth Avenue from luxury convertibles. Popular images of American heroes in cars – movie stars, ball players, singers, astronauts and politicians – were always in convertibles. The Pace Car of the Indianapolis 500, the world's biggest auto racing event, was almost always a convertible, and the model chosen to pace the Memorial Day race was the most photographed American car of the year.

But the total number of convertibles was always low. Out of 1.8 million Chevys sold in 1965, only 92 000 were convertibles, even though this was a peak

year. The discomfort of a wind-blown, draughty cockpit and the eventual rattles that plague convertibles always limited their appeal. But this only served to increase the prestige image by holding down sales. Because most people did not have them, convertibles were badges of privilege for those who did.

In the second half of the sixties, convertible sales declined. The overall level of luxury in American cars was rising and there was a new definition of automotive glamour in the sporty two-door pony cars – Mustang, Camaro and Firebird. With long noses and short tails, the pony cars were the first generation of American cars that did not look better as convertibles. A Mustang convertible was the Indy Pace Car in 1964 and a Camaro convertible was chosen in 1968. Nevertheless, the Camaro and the Pontiac Firebird looked better as hardtops. They also functioned better, since solid-topped cars have greater chassis strength and rigidity than convertibles.

As pony car sales climbed in the seventies, convertible sales dwindled – from 17 000 Chevrolet convertibles in 1969, for instance, to only 8350 in 1975, the last year for most US convertibles. When the convertible was

1976 Cadillac Eldorado
The 1976 Cadillac Eldorado was the last in a long line of Cadillac convertibles. When production of that car ended, it seemed to signal the closing of an era. The convertible symbolized the golden allure of the good life in the 1950s. It was the car owned by stars, heroes, celebrities and political leaders. Indianapolis 500 pace cars were convertibles, until Detroit temporarily stopped making them. The end of the convertible era signalled a bend in the road for Cadillac, whose light would dim as America's leading luxury car.

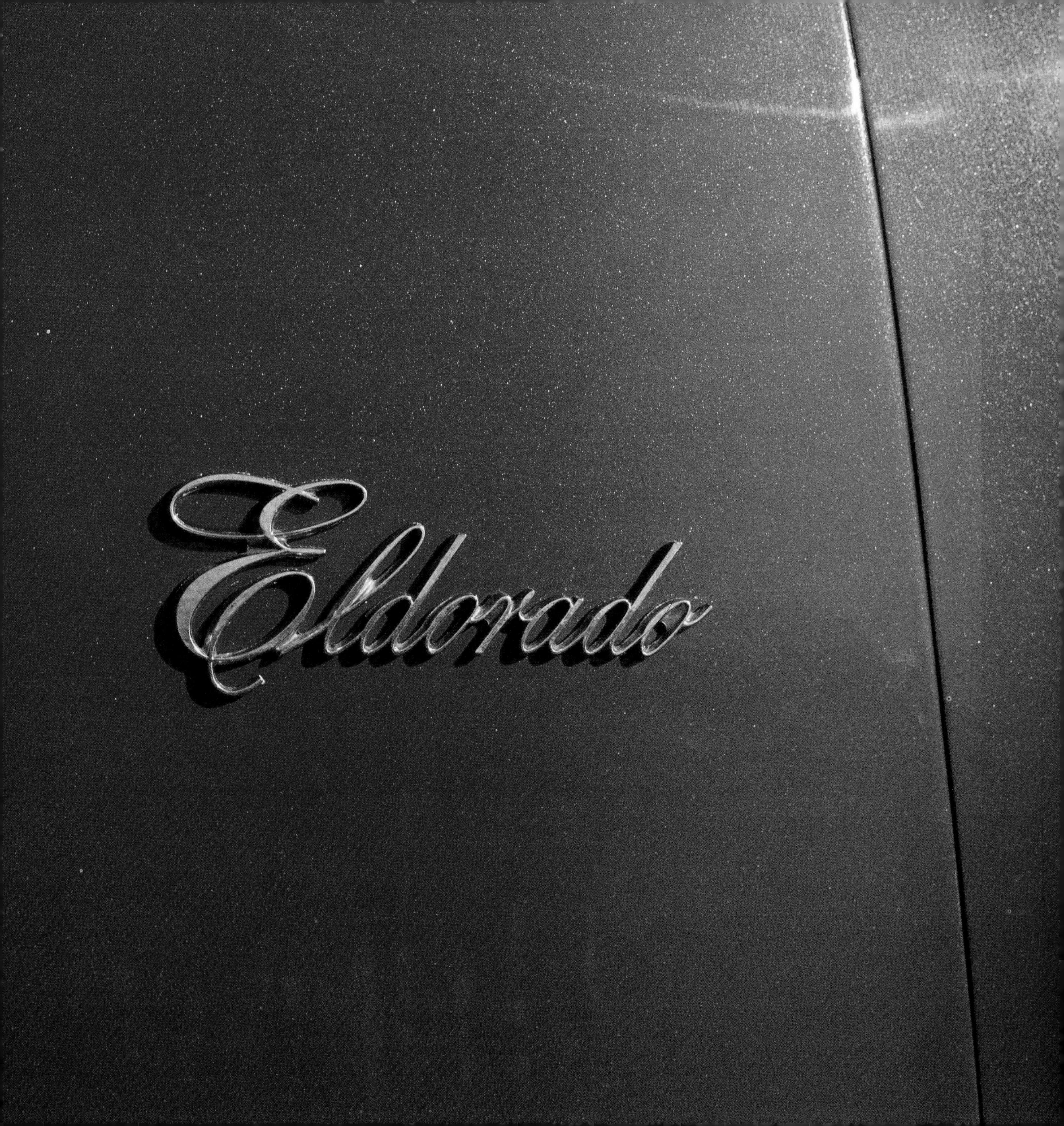
Eldorado

officially declared extinct, if only temporarily, with the 1977 model year, it was a passage more remarked on in the press than in the dealerships where people actually bought cars.

There was already a new expression of style and sport one price level below the pony cars: the front-wheel-drive economy compacts from Japan and Germany. Honda introduced the front-wheel-drive Civic in 1973 and in 1975 Volkswagen introduced the front-wheel-drive Rabbit hatchback to replace the ageing Beetle. The Rabbit and the Civic were cars of changing times, symbols of an apparent shift in techno-logical resources from the United States to Western Europe and Japan. Just as the rear-engine, rear-drive Beetle had been a new concept when it arrived in America in 1949, the front-drive Rabbit and the Civic were technological innovations for the seventies. Cadillac and Oldsmobile were already using front-wheel drive in the Eldorado and Toronado, but the new techno-logy was not employed to change the nature of these cars for the better. The Eldorado and the Toronado were as long and heavy as other GM cars; the techno-logical novelty of front-wheel drive was offered as a luxury feature for those who cared.

VW and Honda offered front-wheel drive for fuel and space economy. The four-cylinder engines of the Rabbit and the Civic were mounted sideways over the front wheels to save weight and space. This layout provided the lightest, most fuel-efficient cars in a market where lightness and fuel efficiency had suddenly become important. Though millions of Americans returned to full-size domestic cars after the first oil price rise, a growing number of people viewed high fuel consumption as a liability and saw gas economy as a benefit – just as they might have gone for V8 power, two-tone vinyl interior and chrome trim in the fifties.

The Civic and the Rabbit were front-wheel-drive compacts at a time when Americans wanted front-wheel-drive compacts. The rear-wheel-drive Vega and Pinto got left behind. The Civic and the Rabbit had new style and new technology. In the past, economy imports had always been low-priced alternatives to the American car. The Honda and the VW were not necessarily cheaper, but now they were perceived as being better than the American competition. Though styling remained a matter of taste, there was no question that the imports performed better.

The Rabbit completely outstripped the performance expectations of an economy car. While the VW Beetle required rowing through the gears to keep up with

1976 Cadillac Eldorado
With its imposing size and dynamic performance, the Eldorado delivered the sense of power and highway dominance millions of Americans wanted in a luxury car. In succeeding years, Cadillac would lose performance and stature through continual down-sizing to meet fuel economy regulations. The Eldorado was the last of the automotive dinosaurs: a huge-engined land cruiser that echoed earlier times when oil was cheap and so was land. It was a car that cried 'Manifest Destiny' and other imperialist American slogans with every contour and chrome accent.

traffic, the Rabbit had power to spare. With 75hp and only 1900 pounds dry weight, the Rabbit's power-to-weight ratio was better than the Porsche Speedster of the fifties. Acceleration and top speed were equal to, if not better than, most American cars that weighed twice as much and looked half as big again. The Rabbit was an astonishing accomplishment in space and weight efficiency, at the same time offering responsive handling and fuel economy.

Lightweight ran against the grain of American taste for big, heavy cars. Weight had always signified value to the American car-buyer. In the fifties, car advertise-ments boasted of 'more road-hugging weight'! An advertisement for the GM compact Corvair in 1960 proclaimed that it handled 'like a heavier car'. Though weight did not improve road-holding in the fifties or any other time, Americans believed it did, and associated the feel of a heavy car with luxury and quality. The exception to that was the lightweight, imported sports car which was enjoyed for superior handling by a more sophisticated and better-informed car buyer. But miniature scale had long been the shape of basic transport in Europe, where gas had always been expensive. Now the Rabbit sold it to Americans adjusting to higher oil prices.

The sparkling performance that made the new

economy compacts so attractive was derived from lightweight construction and overhead-camshaft engine technology. The overhead-valve, overhead-camshaft engines of the Rabbit, the Civic and the Celica were a big step ahead of the overhead-valve, cam-in-block motors that powered the Vega and the Pinto. The overhead-camshaft configuration was as important an advance for engine performance efficiency as the overhead-valve V8 had been for American V8s in the fifties. Locating the camshaft, which operated both exhaust and intake valves, directly above the cylinder head instead of below, provided more positive valve action and better breathing at high engine speed, producing more horsepower.

Just as important as the performance technology, though, was the Rabbit's undeniable, almost flamboyant style. It was no minimalist exercise in mathematical styling that sacrificed aesthetics to expediency. While the VW Beetle had succeeded with a stark, functional shape that made it a statement of anti-style, the Rabbit boasted a chopped, angular box shape that was as modern as the Beetle was old-fashioned. The crisp, dynamic lines came from the ItalDesign studio of Giorgietto Giugiaro, the Italian styling genius behind the DeTomaso Mangusta and the Maserati Bora. The Rabbit was Giugiaro's rendering of the family car to sub-compact size in a bold, original package.

One purpose of front-wheel drive in both Civic and Rabbit was to save interior space by eliminating the driveshaft-transmission tunnel from the engine to the rear wheels found in most rear-drive cars. The front-wheel-drive layout was designed for the largest volume of usable interior space at the lowest gross weight. The Rabbit's modified box front-end was complemented by the double forward-angled rear that was neither fastback nor standard hatchback. Instead, the body line angled forward beneath the rear bumper in a modified vee profile which restated the hatched-off triangle line of the rear window.

Luggage space could have been increased with straight vertical lines to the rear hatch window and the lower rear body panel for a square tail. But that would have created the dull shape of a van like the VW Microbus. Even with its stylish contours, the Rabbit had so much usable space there was no need for more beneath the bumper. The rear seats could be folded flat to expand the small trunk into a huge cargo area, a convertible, modular-space feature in sync with the new reality of American cars. Though the traditional family car had room for six and a trunk full of luggage for trips, the classic Norman Rockwell *Saturday Evening*

Post-cover American family with children, grandparent and dog on vacation was a thing of the past. Most families had more cars and fewer children and seldom needed the seating capacity of a big car.

Everything about the Rabbit was right: the name, the shape, the look, the image. A Rabbit was smart, the automotive counterpart to a pair of running shoes. Like Adidas, which launched athletic shoes as fashion and translated function into style, the Rabbit led a new wave of automotive fashion that made economy and space efficiency chic.

Volkswagen's new image was carried several steps further with the Scirocco, VW's first out-and-out

1970s VW Golf Rabbit
The Rabbit was a new concept for Volkswagen in America. In place of the virtues of economy and praticality came the excitement of the new technology of front-wheel drive together with a spirited performance. Thanks to the design genius of Giorgietto Giugiaro, the Rabbit folded its impressive carrying capacity in a stylish shape that made efficiency chic.

glamour car. Built on the Rabbit platform, the Scirocco was a sporty two-door with the sensuous shape of a GT coupe. Also a Giugiaro design, the Scirocco had the Rabbit's planes and angles lowered and lengthened into a graceful, flowing silhouette. There was no hint of utility or economy in the car's image – only in the price and gas mileage. The Scirocco was Giugiaro's transposition of economy compact engineering into a glamorous, sporty car that completely shed the utility-economy stigma of the low-priced import.

Style was spreading through the Japanese auto model lines as the sporty compact market expanded in the second half of the seventies. The 1977 Toyota

Celica fastback reflected the looks of a miniature 1970 Mustang and the Celica notchback resembled a scaled-down Dodge Challenger. Derivative or not, the Celica capitalized on the appeal of the Mustang and Challenger in a two-door compact with the flair of a sports car without a sports car's drawbacks.

As Japanese and German sub-compacts glamorized the lower level of the American auto business, German and Swedish cars were moving in on a price level above the fully loaded Ford, Chevrolet or Plymouth. Volvo, Saab, Audi and BMW had come to represent taste and sophistication to the Baby-boom generation that had grown up since World War II. These German

The 1977 Rabbit. You've got to drive it to believe it.

1977 VW Golf Rabbit
The Rabbit was the new shape of the family car in America. The Norman Rockwell *Saturday Evening Post* magazine cover family with grandma, the dog and four kids stuffed in the back of a big Detroit sedan was history. The American family of 2.4 children and two cars per household travelled in cars like the Rabbit, but not together.

and Swedish sedans were automotive ID badges for the young, upscale professionals who would later be labelled 'Yuppies'. The upscale Baby Boomers were a prized demographic group of buyers with high education levels, large amounts of spending money and strong influence on the media. Though Yuppies gave almost religious devotion to fashion trends and style in clothes, food, wine, video equipment and skis, they preferred cars that made a virtue out of apparent indifference to fashion. Yuppies favoured conservative, practical-looking mid-size sedans – provided they were made in Germany or Sweden by BMW, Audi, Volvo or Saab and advertised in the *New Yorker* magazine. The

austere, neo-Victorian lines of the Volvo and the strange, stark shape of Saab had the blessing of desirability to a generational group that raised fulfilment of material desire to a spiritual quest. Volvo, Saab, Audi and BMW had sports-performance images from rallying or road racing, but they were built for durability and long-term economy, and they looked it.

Of the four, BMW had the highest performance image, even though its best seller, the entry-level 320, was slower and clumsier than Audi or Saab. Until the success of the 320 as a major American status symbol in the late seventies, BMW had occupied a relatively obscure niche in the US market as a small, plain-looking German car with an enthusiast image. The model that had focused this image in the sixties was the 2002, a two-door, four-and-a-half passenger miniature sedan that performed like a sports car. The 2002 had been created specifically for the American market in 1967 as a European, scaled-down version of the Pontiac GTO. Like the phenomenally successful GTO, the 2002 was created by putting an engine from a larger, more expensive model into an existing two-door sedan – the 1600, a lively and responsive car with a small, devoted following in the United States.

At that time, BMW's image strength came from its motorcycles, a line of sports-touring machines known

for vibration-free operation, superb engineering quality, excellent handling and unparalleled reliability. The 2002 changed all that, remaking BMW's automotive image. A two-litre engine gave the car exciting performance in a space-efficient, if unglamorous, shape at a moderate price of under $3000. The 2002 was irresistible to sports car enthusiasts and got raves in the sports car magazines *Car & Driver* and *Road & Track*. The success of the 2002 as an enthusiast's car carried BMW into the mainstream of the trend-oriented media and signified BMW as a car that had arrived.

When BMW replaced it with the 320 in 1976, the 2002 had gained weight and lost performance to emission, safety and economy regulations. But sales had not been affected, and although the 320 proved to be less of a performer, with more weight and less power at almost three times the price of the original 2002, the image remained the same. Priced between a loaded Chevrolet Monte Carlo and the base model Cadillac Calais, the BMW 320 sold economy-car performance at a luxury-car price. It was the market conquest of a car that offered less for more. Though it was bigger outside, the 320 was smaller inside than the VW Rabbit, which cost less than half as much and could outperform the BMW either in a straight line or on a winding road. BMW's advertising campaign traded on

Left: **1971 BMW 2002 Auto**
Right: **1971 BMW 2002 Turbo**
Conceived especially for the American market, the 2002 was a two-door miniature sedan that performed like a sports car. Like the Mustang and the Pontiac GTO, the 2002 got its sparkling performance from an engine produced for a larger car in the BMW line. With the powerful overhead-camshaft four, the 2002 set a new standard and defined a new category of enthusiast car: the small sports sedan. The 2002 had a distinctly practical, unglamorous shape, with the style reserved for function in the German Bauhaus tradition. The 2002 Turbo was not made in a US export version, but was popular in Britain and on the Continent.

the past racing successes of other BMW models to create a market image of BMW as 'The Ultimate Driving Machine'. The reality behind that image was unimportant to young professionals, who bought BMWs for prestige and pride of ownership, not fast driving. The satisfaction was in believing they owned a superior car, and there was no reason to jeopardize that satisfaction by testing the car against something cheaper and faster like a Rabbit.

The 320 was a simple, unadorned two-door sedan with a modest hood and a short rear deck like a VW Rabbit with a trunk instead of a bob-tail. Like Volvo and Saab, the BMW 320 styling was neither glamorous nor exciting; it was adequate. Yet the 320 was the 'must-have' car for the young attorney, the executive trainee and the accountant who were not put off by the high maintenance and service expenses. They welcomed exorbitant service charges as the price of quality, which is always expensive. The more it costs, the more it can be believed to be worth. The BMW 320 was the triumph of an image which became the symbol of success for the young professional who could not yet afford a Mercedes-Benz. Rabbits and

Hondas might be chic, but they did not confer status on their owners. BMWs did.

Like Porsche and Mercedes-Benz, BMW achieved its greatest gains in the American market and mind during years of drastic economic realignment between dollar and Deutsche Mark. The inflation and recession years of the seventies in America led to a continuing decline in the strength of the dollar against the Mark. By 1980, German prices in America had tripled in a decade. German car sales in the US market increased during those years almost as much as prices did, reflecting a new trend: buying for the prestige of price. In a society where the automobile was the most visible and variable status symbol, it was simple arithmetic that a Mercedes-Benz SL roadster, which climbed from $10 000 to $30 000 between 1970 and 1980, had more prestige clout than a Cadillac Eldorado which began the decade as an $8000 car and ended it at $18 000.

The shift of an important flavour in American taste from domestic to imported prestige cars happened during the years author Tom Wolfe labelled 'The Me Decade', for the attention Americans paid to short-

1970s BMW 320
The 2002 had established BMW as a new automotive status symbol in the US before it was replaced by the 320. A fuller, more rounded shape with a suggestion of streamlining, the 320 was the right car for the American Yuppie at the tail end of the seventies and the beginning of the eighties. It was overpriced, underpowered, offered mediocre road performance but had unmatchable status cachet for the upwardly mobile buyer who could not yet afford a Mercedes. The BMW 320 and the blue, black and white emblem became a trademark of American Yuppie-dom for the 1980s.

term courses in self-improvement, health, wealth and success. It was a time of heavy spending on clothes, food, home video and audio equipment, real estate and cars. The more expensive the car, the more desirable it was. Though the British pound had not shifted against the dollar like the Deutsche Mark, Rolls-Royce correctly read the market and adjusted prices upwards to keep well above Mercedes-Benz in cost. As the most expensive car on the road, Rolls-Royce became an attractive car to people who had over-looked it when it cost less.

In Beverly Hills, the home of America's most cherished movie, TV and recording stars, status was almost entirely a matter of money. For entertainers, it was measured by the multiple of the millions of dollars grossed per year. For cars it was simply a matter of price. That made the Rolls-Royce Corniche convertible, up to an impressive $90 000 mark by 1979, the premier status car in Los Angeles. Also popular, though less numerous, were the $60 000 Lamborghini Countach and the Ferrari Boxer, which shared the claim to being the world's fastest street car. The Italian supercars were to speed what the Rolls-Royce was to price and luxury – the most of both. But the Corniche and the Italian 12-cylinder supercars were so far beyond the reach of most wallets they were not many people's dream cars. The legend of the Shelby Cobra survived as the last word in high performance; the Cobra was the fast car that was craved by the most people.

Then, in 1976, Porsche rearranged the pieces in the high-performance game with a super-911 called the Turbo Carrera. Priced at $26 000, the Turbo Carrera was a pumped-up, styled-up, souped-up 911 with 50 per cent more power thanks to the magic of turbo-charging. Using energy from otherwise wasted exhaust pressure, the turbocharger is a pump that compresses the fuel-air mixture before combustion, creating a bigger, more powerful explosion. Though GM had tried turbocharging with the Chevy Corvair and the Olds F085 in the sixties, the Turbo Carrera was the first successful turbocharged street car. The turbo Porsche was the expensive product of complex engin-eering that turned an already fast car into a rocket. It was a rich man's muscle car with a German accent, at triple the price of a Corvette. Like its blue-collar American muscle car counterparts – the Mustang Boss 302, the Camaro Z28 and the Plymouth 'Cuda AAR 340 – the Turbo Carrera had heavy-duty suspension, competition brakes and flared fenders to accommodate special extra-wide wheels and tyres. The Turbo had

1985 Lamborghini Countach

An overheated economy and a growing number of millionaires put an amazing number of megabucks supercars on the streets in the late seventies. Cars that cost the price of houses, with speeds more commonly associated with aeroplanes, became the new status performance cars. Most exotic of the lot was the Countach, a car with a near unpronounceable name and a devastating shape. No one seemed concerned that it was almost impossible to see anything except what was directly ahead when driving a Countach. What mattered, apparently, was how the Countach looked to others. The profile alone was probably worth the price, which started at well under $100 000 and climbed higher. The Ferrari Boxer cost as much as the Countach and boasted a higher top speed. But the mean, purposeful shape of the Ferrari lacked the blatant sex appeal of the Countach, and the Boxer never matched the Lamborghini in all-out exotic mystique.

special trim and a brutal-looking rear airfoil, nicknamed the 'whale-tail', for stability at over 150 mph.

Though it cost less than half as much as the 12-cylinder Italian supercars, the Porsche Turbo Carrera could out-accelerate either the Lamborghini Countach or the Ferrari Boxer. It could humiliate a Corvette in a street race and the once-proud Corvette driver learned to look the other way when a Porsche pulled alongside at a light. In full-bulge fender-flare, fat-tyred stance with front spoiler and whale-tail, the formerly mild-looking Porsche had metamorphosed into a Teutonic warlock of the street. It was the absolute performance king up to its 160 mph top speed, the

1975 Porsche 911 Turbo Carrera

The Porsche Turbo was much more than an exotic performance car. It offered quarter-mile acceleration and zero-to-60 speed to whip any Detroit muscle car packaged in a plush *gran turisimo* style.

cruising velocity of a light plane.

The Turbo Carrera opened a new chapter in the book of performance supercars. Unlike the speed monsters that preceded it, such as the Cobra 427, the Corvette 427 and the Dodge hemi-Charger, the Turbo Carrera did not sacrifice comfort for speed. The cockpit was as quiet, cool and comfortable as that in a non-turbocharged 911, an exceptionally comfortable sports car. Turbocharging gave the Carrera a dual personality that could switch from Clark Kent to Superman mode any moment. At part throttle, the Turbo Carrera operated on a non-boosted engine, which provided quiet, even-tempered quickness

performance was available without the encumbrance of a punishing ride, the intrusive noise of a bad-mannered engine and an overheated cockpit. The Turbo Carrera combined fighter-plane performance with luxury-car comfort. Though Carreras were rare machines on the street, they received consistent raves in enthusiast magazines that made them the extremists' dream car and established Porsche as a major auto-motive force in the American performance world.

The big-block American performance car was widely believed to be past its time, consigned to history by changing tastes and shifting economic priorities. But the Pontiac Trans-Am was still the frontline car for the regular American speed-lover in 1978, with a 400 cubic-inch V8 keeping the tradition alive. Mustang had introduced a new car for 1978, with another new shape and a selection of engine choices that included a four, a six, a turbocharged four and the tried-and-trusty V8. Chevrolet had dropped the Z28 edition of the Camaro and Chrysler discontinued the V8 as a performance engine altogether, but Ford elected to keep V8 performance going until it was clinically dead on the market.

Detroit was getting confusing signals. The public had panicked again when a second oil crisis in the late seventies drove gasoline prices skyward and brought on a renewed clamour for small economy cars. In response, Ford introduced a new front-wheel-drive sub-compact called the Escort, Chrysler brought out the sub-compact, front-wheel-drive Omni-Horizon, and General Motors introduced the compact, front-wheel-drive X-car family.

The second gasoline price rise had also sparked interest in diesel-engined cars as a hedge against further oil price inflation. Diesel fuel was cheaper than gasoline and diesel cars got more miles per gallon than gasoline-engined cars. But diesel cars had serious drawbacks. They were sluggish and slow to start in cold weather. They smoked at idle and rattled under acceleration. Mercedes-Benz had been selling diesel passenger cars worldwide since the thirties and their 240D had a small, low-profile image in the United States. The plain-lined, no-frills 240D was a utility-car stepchild in a luxury-car family, the sole non-status Mercedes-Benz on the US market.

The diesel engine cast off its industrial image in 1978 when Mercedes-Benz turbocharged it, installed it under the hood of an elegant sedan and christened it the Turbodiesel SD. The new 300SD Turbodiesel was fast, quiet, quick-starting, elegant, expensive and thrifty

without overheating, exhaust crackle or the lumpy, galloping idle displayed by most hyper-performance cars in traffic. Full throttle cranked on the boost, spiking the power curve and turning the Carrera into a launched missile.

But even full bore, the Turbo Carrera maintained a quiet interior comfort level. It had more luxurious carpeting and trim than the standard 911, with the most sophisticated and elaborate climate control and stereo systems available. It had electrically adjustable outside rearview mirrors with heated glass to prevent fogging, and washing jets to clean the headlight lenses of bugs and road grit at speed. For once, the ultimate

all at once. For a satisfying $30 000 it delivered good, if not great, mileage, on fuel that cost less than gasoline. That made the Turbodiesel perfect for the affluent liberal who wanted luxury without guilt over the profligacy of a V8 that delivered driving pleasure by squandering the world's energy resources. With luxury-car styling and turbocharged performance, the 300SD made diesel chic.

Others jumped in on the act. VW brought out a diesel Rabbit, Peugeot marketed an American diesel sedan while Cadillac and Oldsmobile produced diesels that looked like American luxury cars, performed like VW Beetles and sounded like buses. If the fad had lasted, GM would have extended diesel down to the medium and lower-priced lines. But to overcome the negative image of diesel, GM started out at the top of the family tree with Cadillac and Oldsmobile. Though it was widely believed that gasoline prices would continue to climb, the escalation halted just past the $1-a-gallon point in 1979, almost four times the pump price in 1972. Once gas prices stabilized, the auto market settled down and the diesel fad died.

While European influences on engineering, styling and performance were shaping some areas of the American auto market, the old-fashioned American pick-up truck was becoming the trend of the late

seventies. The pick-up had been popular since the fifties when it came into widespread use by farmers, small-time building contractors and men who worked with tools or hauled materials for a living. In the sixties, pick-ups began attracting buyers who did not need them for work but drove them for transport because they preferred a truck to a car.

Brawny, tough, hard-riding and powerful, pick-up trucks were rugged, heavy-duty vehicles for the oilfield worker, the ranch-hand, the southern saw-mill worker in the fifties and sixties. In the seventies, when car engines were getting smaller, European and Oriental cars were coming over and American cars were losing power to regulatory controls, the big American pick-up truck became a four-wheeled masculinity symbol. If cars were changing in response to unpleasant shifts in the global balance of power, pick-up trucks were the same tough American machine they had always been. Trucks became part of the pop culture of the seventies in the same wave that carried cowboy boots, Western hats, dungarees, Waylon Jennings and Willie Nelson into the American mainstream. It could have been called Cowboy Chic or Truck Chic, except cowboys and truckers did not use French words. Trucks were all-American vehicles. If the country was turning to city, with suburbs wiping out the rural backland, trucks

Left: **1977 Dodge Pickup**
Right: **1976 Dodge Ramcharger SE**
Truck love swept America in the seventies in a romance that spoke to the latent asphalt cowboy spirit. Big, tough and brawny, trucks evoked the rugged frontier spirit that was part of the American heritage. Broncos, Blazers and Ramchargers with oversized tyres, roof racks, light bars and off-road equipment were part of a new cultural wave that carried the country music of Waylon Jennings and Willie Nelson into mainstream America. The 4X4 trucks were part of a new wave of cowboy chic and a celebration of macho on wheels.

were the wheels of the asphalt cowboy and the highway the home of the brave.

By the late seventies full-size American pick-up trucks were outselling most American sedans, with four million trucks sold in 1978. Truck popularity was booming when the actual need for trucks was less than ever. Most of their duties could be done more efficiently by other vehicles, but trucks symbolized a rugged, ornery sense of independence and self-reliance that was an important aspect of American character. A pick-up truck dominated its territory on the road and made a clear statement. Pick-up truck-driving was best enjoyed with a Willie Nelson-Waylon Jennings cassette on the stereo, an extra sixpack of Budweiser in the cooler and a Winchester in the gun-rack behind the seat in plain sight.

Pick-ups were fun to drive. The Dodge Ram had V8 power after V8s had been dropped from most Chrysler cars; the big-block Ford 429 and the Chevy 454 were still available in Ford, Chevy and GMC pick-ups. The power and heft belonged to the cultural heritage of post-war America, part of the nostalgic wave in pop music and movies of the early seventies that raised the tractor-trailer truck driver to folk hero. Pick-up trucks were the closest most Americans would get to the romance of the big rigs, and in the seventies more people were driving them than ever.

1970s Mazda B200 Pickup
Mini-trucks were a Japanese innovation for the American market, and were welcomed into the American automotive family with the warmth usually reserved for a sports car. They became the mini-rage of the seventies.

The pick-up truck passion clashed with the current economics and the prevailing fashion and design winds from Europe. The pick-up is a uniquely American vehicle that has remained basically unchanged in shape or layout since it evolved as a variation on the sedan in the twenties. Utility trucks in other countries are snub-nosed, cab-over vehicles that make maximum use of space. The pick-up configuration, which wastes space in front of the cab and over the open bed, evolved when gasoline was too cheap for concern about efficient space utilization. The layout never changed.

The Ford F-100, the Chevy Step-side and the Dodge Ram made concessions to the seventies with smooth lines and rounded edges. But the truck shape - with a small enclosed cab, an extended hood and a large, open bed with unusable space above it — was the heart of the pick-up's appeal. The pick-up truck driver and passenger looked down on the roofs of cars and did not look up at anybody — except tractor-trailer trucks, the biggest machines on the road.

Though pick-up trucks were increasingly refined through the fifties and sixties in the direction of sedan comfort and convenience, a truck still imposed a huge compromise in comfort and convenience over a car. A truck cab has much less usable space than even a two-seat sports car, because there is no temporary storage area behind the seats. Pick-up truck ride is stiffer and more jarring than cars, and the ride is harsher unloaded

Mazda B2000 Pickups
The more you look, the more you like.

than loaded. Since most Americans use trucks not for hauling but for transport or recreational driving, the beds are usually empty. That means the hauling space is wasted and the ride is hard. But a rough ride and wasted space were just what millions of Americans wanted to put on the road, and pick-up trucks were their answer.

The van was another utility vehicle that became popular as a personal transport in the seventies. Vans lack the handsome, macho image of the pick-up truck, the performance of a V8 sedan and the sportiness of a

1977 Dodge Van
The rectangular contour of the van became the new shape of the American recreation vehicle in the seventies. Vans made by Dodge, Ford and GM were the late seventies' counterpart to the VW Microbus of the sixties.

compact. Yet, neither car nor truck, they became so popular with young Americans that, inevitably, there was a movie called *The Van*. Just as counter-culturists and hippies found independence and freedom in the VW Microbus in the sixties, teenagers of the late seventies formed a lifestyle around vans. The vogue with vans was wild custom-painted exteriors and interiors outfitted in the style of a Las Vegas luxury motel suite. Mega-watt, multi-speaker stereo music systems were mandatory van appliances, along with a Citizen's Band shortwave radio and a cooler or a small

New Dodge Street Van

For you van fans, a basic vehicle that's something else. Plus some far-out ideas about going your own way.
Your way sums up the whole Dodge Street Van plan. That's why…as you can see here…we provide you with a vehicle that's highly individualistic to begin with; an ideal basis for adding all the goodies you want, to make it yours, like nothing else on the road.

High-back Command bucket seats, carpeting, road wheels, fat tires, and more.
First, the standard Street Van exterior gives you a lot of custom bright trim in the right places—on front grille surround moulding, front and rear bumpers, windshield moulding, tail lamp bezels, and side mirrors.

Then, you get extra pizzazz on the inside; big, new high-back Command bucket seats with fold-down armrests upholstered in sharp Boca Raton cloth and vinyl. Choose blue, green, parchment, or saddle. And there are added dress-up items like carpeting, padded instrument panel with simulated wood grain insert, and color-keyed vinyl door trim panels with simulated wood-grain.

Finally, we put the whole rig on your choice of either five-slot chrome disc road wheels or white painted spoke road wheels—and add fat H70 x 15-B raised white letter tires. Note: It may be necessary to secure some of the equipment items pictured here through customizing shops.

4

'Love Vans'
Vanning quickly became part of the subculture, with van clubs and cults attracting teenagers everywhere. Vans were outfitted with bars, stereos and bordello-style upholstery. They became freedom on wheels for teenagers, mobile havens that parents and authorities suspected were dens of dope, wild music and sex.

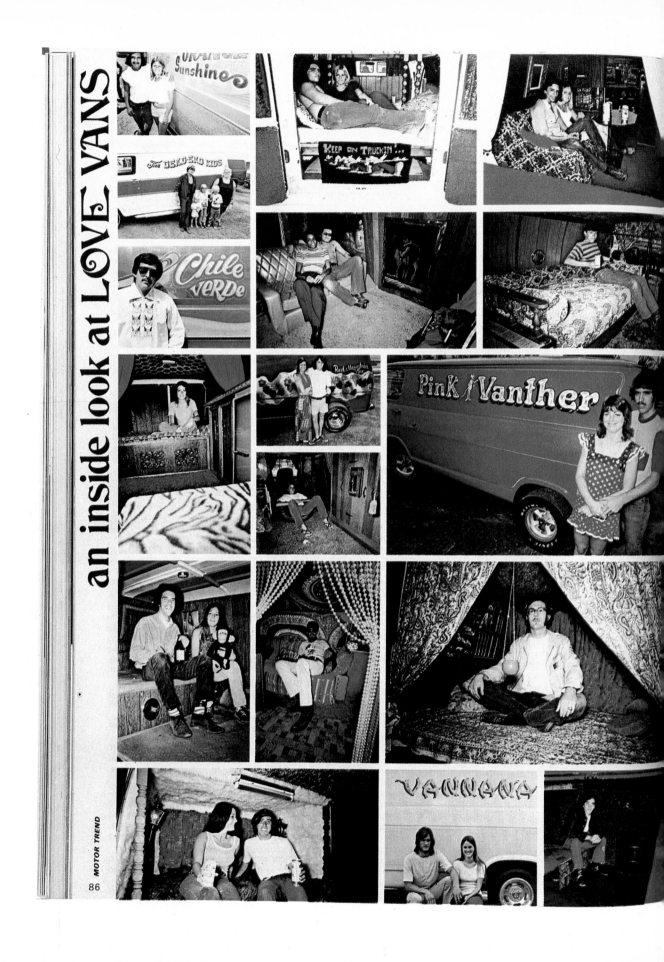

an inside look at LOVE VANS

MOTOR TREND

86

162

refrigerator to keep the beer cold.

More than pick-ups, the van became a sub-cultural icon for teenagers in the seventies, with van clubs and weekend drive-ins and over-the-road communication through CB radio. The styles of West Coast customizing of the fifties reappeared on vans that were lowered in front, trimmed with front spoilers, fender flaps, custom louvres, tinted glass and hand-painted murals and tapestry designs. Vans were an identity symbol that marked teenagers as members of a group clearly separate from the grown-up world. The luxury of appliances and stereo system gave them a sense of comfort and security away from the rules laid down by adults. With music, drinks and drugs on board, vans were sex on wheels.

The love of trucks that lay behind the van and pick-up truck trends of the seventies made it almost inevitable that someone would miniaturize the pick-up to make it even more popular. The Japanese mini-pick-up of the seventies was just that: a miniature pick-up truck in an economical, up-to-date format looking forward to the eighties. Offering pick-up truck appeal, sports-compact performance, sub-compact fuel economy and price, the mini-pick-up was an instant hit on both the East and West coasts. Mini-trucks made by Mazda, Toyota and Datsun were popular as economical light-duty haulers, as a second or third family car, and as sport trucks for teenagers.

For the younger generation, mini-pick-ups were made to order. They had the rebel, bad-boy image of the big trucks at a little-truck price. They got great performance with the overhead-cam engines from Japanese sports compacts, and in California they practically begged to be customized with flared fenders, spoke wheels and wide tyres, front spoilers, tinted windows, custom pipes, interiors and paint jobs. Mini-trucks could be wild street customs with colour stripes and lowered front ends; they could be trick campers with enclosed box beds; they could be mini-macho off-road chargers with oversized tyres, hijacker shocks, light racks and roll bars. They could be mini-road racers, lowered front and rear with front air dam, side skirts and modified engine.

Clubs sprang up for mini-truck lovers of all persuasions. Minis were badges of 'belonging' for teenagers who believed the trucks had been created specially for them. Mini-trucks were a fad that eventually turned into a main thread of American automobile culture, thanks to a Japanese innovation which launched a new American tradition.

THE EARLY EIGHTIES

Ferrari's TV stardom,
the DeLorean nightmare and the rebirth
of the American V8

Ferrari starred on the TV detective series *Magnum, P.I.* and *Miami Vice* as the ultimate stylish car for America's favourite screen bachelors. Television boosted Ferrari's dream car status when Cadillac, Lincoln and Corvette had fallen behind Mercedes-Benz, BMW and Porsche. The DeLorean dashed a million hopes for a great new American car, revealing itself as the American nightmare on wheels. Japan, Germany and Sweden raised style and performance levels in small, high-tec designs while Cadillac lost all pretence of performance and styling leadership. The Ford Mustang GT signalled the comeback of American V8 performance with a computer-modulated motor to challenge Porsche and Ferrari. The new Lincoln Mark VII revitalized the American luxury performance car and the Corvette was born again in a brilliant new design with world-class performance.

FERRARI finally became an American dream car in the eighties. Not by winning sports car races, which made it the most desired sports car in Europe. Not by rolling up successive Grand Prix Formula One championships, which made it an international auto-racing legend. Ferrari reached dream car status in America by the national medium of success – television. As the starring vehicle in two hit TV series – *Magnum, P.I.* and *Miami Vice* – the exotic Ferrari shape became a familiar sight in American living rooms. The cars in the shows – a 308GTS and a Daytona Spyder – were not cast for speed or performance, but as fashion accessories to a pair of glamorous undercover detectives. The TV shows and their leading men were so popular that their Ferraris became a new vision of the ultimate car for millions of American TV watchers.

It marked the top of a long upward climb for the American TV detective's car since the fifties, when the TV cop car was a plain Ford sedan and Ferrari was the plaything of princes, playboys and movie stars. In the fifties, the blunt, unhandsome Jack Webb played the unsmiling Sergeant Friday on TV's *Dragnet* in cheap, off-the-rack suits and sports clothes that matched the economy Ford police car. That was when the word millionaire held a magical aura of rarity and the rich were considered different. In the sixties, the image of glamour on wheels was played by the Corvette in *Route 66* and America's favourite fictional undercover operative was James Bond, who drove a gold Aston Martin DB7.

By the late seventies, there were too many American millionaires to be counted. A long-running bull market in real estate and investment trading had swelled the net worth of enough people to blur the line between the merely wealthy and the downright rich was blurred. The leading men on the television of the eighties were fashion-forward undercover detectives who wore jewellery and designer sportswear, carried designer guns and drove designer cars. It was inevitable that Ferrari would follow Mercedes-Benz and Porsche into the American car consciousness.

By the eighties, the ultimate in automotive style for America's TV heroes was no longer found in Detroit. It had to be European; in fact, it had to be Italian. Porsche could have done the job as an automobile, but its image was not sufficiently exotic because there were

1972 Ferrari Daytona Spyder
The Ferrari Daytona became the American dream car of the eighties through a starring role in the hit TV series *Miami Vice*, and a Daytona was also featured in the light road-farce *Gumball Rally* (below). The Daytona, with the sleek, sensual styling of Pininfarina at his best, was well equipped for stardom. It was the last V12 front-engined two-seat sports car from Ferrari. A 170 mph top speed made the Daytona the absolute performance king of the road.

Left: 1972 Ferrari Daytona Spyder
The convertible spyder added sex appeal that hiked the Spyder's value as a collector's car to over $500 000 in the late 1980s. When new, the Spyder sold for $30 000.

Right: the Spyder used as an undercover vice-squad cop car on *Miami Vice*, and which made the Ferrari marque famous to middle America, was a fake: an imitation Spyder body on a Corvette chassis, with a recording of the Ferrari V12 engine used for the soundtrack instead of the Corvette V8.

Below right: Ferrari's TV stardom began as the glamorous street car of America's most glamorous TV detective of the seventies: Tom Selleck, the star of *Magnum, P.I.*

too many Porsches on the road. The two leading supercars left were Ferrari and Lamborghini, and Lamborghini would not do because the Countach is a coupe and TV stars need to be seen. That meant convertibles, which meant Ferrari.

The Daytona Spyder in *Miami Vice* – played by a replica made with an imitation body on a Corvette chassis – was the ultimate sports car when it starred in the show, just as it had been when it was new ten years earlier. Though it had been out of production since 1973, the Daytona mystique had been enhanced with time and the car increased in value many times over its original $35 000 price. By 1983, the Daytona had become a prized collector's car and the Spyder convertible, of which less than 200 were made, had achieved near art-object status. It was very fast art.

As the last of the Ferrari V12 sports cars, the Daytona was the ultimate in automotive performance luxury, with the technological richness of a double-overhead-camshaft V12 when most performance sports models made do with six or eight cylinders. The Daytona had an extraordinarily graceful Pininfarina body sculpted out of aluminium by Scaglietti. The casting of such a high-toned exotic in the role of an undercover cop's car in *Miami Vice* was only half as silly as it sounds. The Ferrari was supposed to be one of

the spoils of drug enforcement seizure – the confiscated prize of a convicted drug lord – and thus beyond the reach of even the ordinary rich.

The Daytona was well cast as the ultimate sports car; the Ferrari performance cars that came after it, like the Boxer 512, lacked the Daytona's charisma. The Boxer cost much more than the Daytona and had a mid-mounted 12-cylinder engine, which made it as fast if not faster than the Daytona. But the Boxer was an ungainly-looking car with mean, purposeful styling that lacked the sensuous beauty of the Daytona. The Boxer could perhaps have been a starring villain's car, but never the hero's.

The V8-powered 308GTS in *Magnum* was another kind of Ferrari altogether. At $50 000 to $60 000, depending on the year, it was within the price range of the dentists and investment advisors and public relations executives and attorneys who drove cars that cost more than the average American house had sold for a dozen years earlier. The 308GTS was more expensive than a Jaguar XJ6 or a Porsche 928 or a BMW 633, but not so much more as to be out of the question. The difference in cost between the Ferrari and the Mercedes

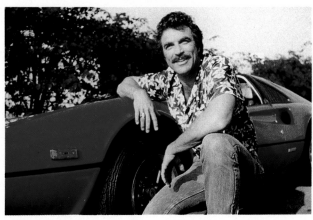

500 SEC was small enough to come down to a choice in style for those who could afford either. The TV role of the 308 in *Magnum* was very close to the real-life part played by the same car – a flashy automotive trophy for the guy who wears Guccis and a gold Rolex and likes to look good on wheels.

The 308GTB (the coupe version of the 308GTS) was Ferrari's entry-level two-seater for the second half of the seventies, a V8-powered effort to meet the crowd slightly less than halfway below the lofty price of the 12-cylinder cars. It launched a new concept of Ferrari as a V8-powered sports car, and broke the Ferrari tradition of presenting ultimate performance at

1976 Ferrari 308GTB
and overleaf
The 308GTB was a clean break from the V12 tradition of Ferrari sports cars for the street. With a V8 engine instead of the traditional V12, the 308GTB offered less excitement at a less spectacular price than the Daytona. The 308GTB caught the rising wave of American status car buying in the 1970s to succeed in a market where looks, name, price and image counted for more than performance. As the first large-volume Ferrari, the 308GTB was a mid-engined car, with the V8 mounted behind the passenger compartment, ahead of the rear wheels. On paper, this was the ideal configuration for high-performance road-holding, but in reality it produced twitchy handling characteristics best utilized by racing drivers on the track. The V8 did not produce enough horsepower to make the 308GTB, or the later Si Spyder version, as exciting a car as it appeared. But for the American status car enthusiast, satisfaction lay in the prestige of owning such a vehicle rather than in its performance. The Ferrari 308GTB had as much style as anything on the road, even if it didn't have the speed to live up to the flash.

the ultimate price. The 308 had the fabled sensuality of design and body contour expected of Ferrari, without the performance. This was a new departure for a car that had been known as the ultimate road car since the fifties, when Ferraris cost as much as Rolls-Royce and could outperform anything on the street. Though seldom seen on American roads in those days, Ferrari meant speed to people who knew the name. The factory racing programme kept that image alive through the sixties, although Ferrari performance was challenged by Corvette on the street and beaten on the track by the AC Cobra.

By 1970, the Cobra was history and the 170 mph Daytona that arrived in the United States that year could easily outrun any Corvette on the road. It could also outperform the Porsche 911S and even the fabled 1973 Carrera RS. It was the fastest street car ever from Ferrari and the 12-cylinder Boxer that followed it was equally fast.

But the car that made it to US streets in sufficient numbers to be noticed was the V8-powered 308 which was a throwback in terms of performance. On paper, the 308GTB sounded fast. It had a double-overhead-camshaft V8 transverse-mounted amidships behind the driver and passenger seats for optimum handling. The Pininfarina styling was lush, voluptuary line at its Italian best. But the car was too heavy for the horsepower and the 1980 308GTB was slower than the less expensive Porsche 911 Carrera, the Porsche 928S or the Porsche 944 Turbo. And the 308GTSi Spyder, which cost as much as the Porsche Turbo Carrera, was not even in the same league as the top-line Porsche for either acceleration or top speed. The 308GTSi was no quicker than a Corvette; in fact, it could not even out-accelerate a used Pontiac Trans-Am in good condition.

Nevertheless, the Ferrari mystique was strong enough to sustain a car that could not win a street fight. Image was what counted, and Ferrari had more performance image than almost any other car. The 308GTSi had the advantage of high price along with sumptuous good looks to boost its status appeal, and all the elements combined to make the topless 308GTSi Spyder the right car for the right time. From its introduction in 1978, the GTS was an immediate hit in southern California. In the upper market levels where the Ferrari V8 was sold, performance was secondary to image, and the Ferrari image outshone the other cars in its price class.

If the Ferrari V8 seemed a different sort of car from

1976 Ferrari 308GTB
The 308GTB was part of a real estate speculation boom that saw condos, gold Rolex watches and Ferraris become part of the landscape of high-dollar sections of major American cities. The 308GTB was a new sort of Ferrari that attracted a new sort of buyer – many of them men who leased their cars rather than buying them outright, which had always been the traditional form of Ferrari ownership. The influx of new money and new Ferrari drivers led to a strong market in Los Angeles and elsewhere for used Ferraris turned in at the end of their leases or before by people anxious to move on to something new. The 308GTB was the first Ferrari to become a familiar sight in used car lots near high-income shopping areas like Beverly Hills.

the legendary V12s of the fifties and sixties, so were the people driving them. In the fifties, Ferraris belonged to the Aga Khan, King Hassan, Prince Bernhard, Porfirio Rubirosa, Roberto Rossellini and Ingrid Bergman. It is hard to believe that those Ferraris were paid for with anything other than cash. But in the seventies the mushrooming popularity of expensive cars matched the increase in the practice of leasing, rather than buying cars. Leasing made it possible for people to drive cars they could not afford to buy. The car still belonged to the bank or lending association after the three- or four-year term of the lease was finished, and the operator of the car had spent $800 or $900 a month for the use of the car and the right to call it his own. At the end of the lease the money spent entitled the person to purchase the car for far less than it was worth. But by then the car was used, and most leaseholders moved on to something new. Auto leasing had tax convenience for many businesses and some individuals, which is what made it popular in the first place. But it appealed to many as a means of driving a car too expensive for them to buy, and the fact that money was paid as rental rather than equity was not important. What mattered was driving the right car, and in the eighties Ferrari was one of the right cars. Nowhere in the United States was there more business in leasing expensive cars than southern California, and the Ferrari 308GTB and GTS became as familiar on Los Angeles streets in the eighties as Porsche had been in the sixties.

No time could have been better than the beginning of the eighties for the arrival of a speciality car like the DeLorean, yet it was to prove a dismal automotive farce that rivalled the Edsel in sheer magnitude of failure. Reams of favourable publicity preceded the DeLorean to the waiting dealer showrooms of Los Angeles, where a weird assortment of other off-brand vehicles had already been sold at extraordinarily high prices to people who were anxious to believe the cars were fine art, as the makers claimed.

Named Clenet, Dinapoli, Zimmer and other imaginative titles, the speciality cars were built in a distorted, ersatz thirties style on seventies American car chassis

1981 DeLorean
The DeLorean arrived on the US market to the greatest hype surrounding any car in memory. Created by the quasi-brilliant John DeLorean, it was awaited as an automotive saviour in a lack-lustre domestic market. The DeLorean looked like a winner.

salvaged from junkyards. The bodies of these creations were overblown statements of automotive fantasy with sweeping fenders, headlamps the size of search-lights, chrome gewgaws and gargoyles and crustaceous trim on every surface. Sold in numbered lots like the limited-edition imitation collector items marketed by the Franklin Mint, they were eagerly bought for $50 000 or $60 000 and driven with pride by people willing to overlook second-rate engineering, comfort and reliability in view of the satisfyingly high price and the pride of owning a brand-new antique. Most, but not all, of the speciality car businesses had failed by the time John Z. DeLorean unleashed his own speciality car on a wider scale than any of the other operators had dared contemplate.

Though the neo-classic speciality cars were snickered at by enthusiasts and automotive journalists as silly toys of the silly nouveau riche, the DeLorean was treated with a seriousness completely out of proportion to its merits. As head of Pontiac before moving to Chevrolet, DeLorean had taken full credit for the production and success of the GTO. He was an executive star for the automotive news media when he left General Motors in 1973 to build a car that would remedy everything wrong with Detroit. Though half of the seventies was gone before the plan was in place, DeLorean's promise to deliver the Second Coming of the automobile was taken seriously.

The early seventies were a low-water period for the American performance car, a time when people had a need to believe in someone like DeLorean. The car was easy to believe in. Designed by Giugiaro and built by Lotus, it would combine state-of-the-art performance engineering with a shape by the finest hand in automotive design. It would have everything a supercar needed but a potent engine, and there were

1981 DeLorean
The DeLorean styling was the work of the brilliant Italian stylist Giorgietto Guigiaro. Derivative of the Lotus Esprit, also a Giugiaro design, the DeLorean looked enticing, with a sensuous Italian body on a car designed by the genius Colin Chapman, creator of Lotus sports and racing cars. The gull-wing doors were an aesthetic indulgence which harked back to the excitement of the legendary 1955 Mercedes-Benz 300SL.

1981 DeLorean
Stunning to look at, the DeLorean's styling turned out to be the only praiseworthy feature of the car. In every other respect, it was a spectacular failure. In operation, the DeLorean was a trouble-prone, ill-handling, under-powered, unreliable, uncomfortable disaster.

rumours that the V6 engine would be turbocharged for a world-beating performance version. The scale of manufacturing for the DeLorean dwarfed any previous speciality car effort and made the extent of the failure all the more spectacular. As a failure, the DeLorean surpassed almost every independent automotive production venture in history.

The car was set up to be a triumph of independent entrepreneurship over entrenched corporate bureaucracy in a commercial replay of the American Revolution, with John Z. DeLorean as the fearless rebel leader. Earlier independent efforts by Preston Tucker, Briggs Cunningham, Bill Devin, Lance Reventlow and even Malcolm Bricklin had been noble failures to varying degrees, inspiring admiration and affection for valiant efforts that failed mainly through being too expensive to compete with mass-produced cars. These earlier one-man cars delivered what their makers promised, but cost too much to succeed. The DeLorean flopped on its own merits, failing to match the minimum standards of quality or performance of even the dullest and cheapest cars on the market.

The DeLorean finally arrived in 1981, after several years of delays, to a buyers' market almost breathless with anticipation. America's favourite TV host Johnny Carson was an investor in the DeLorean, and thousands of Americans were waiting their turn to spend the price of a Mercedes on an American car – if a car built in Ireland with an Italian body on an English chassis with a French engine could be considered American. The stunning silver shape of the DeLorean had been seen in photographs almost as often as Bo Derek, who was dominating magazine and tabloid picture space at the time. There was no question about the DeLorean's beauty. The design by Giugiaro was similar to the Lotus Esprit, which was a stunning car. In the brushed silver finish of the unpainted steel body, the DeLorean shape at least justified hyperbole.

The DeLorean arrived in the United States to a level of expectation which probably equalled the expectation preceding the Edsel and the Mustang. DeLorean's long and skilful public relations campaign for himself and the car had kept the press on his side, and the enthusiast magazines supported the car even though it failed many of the standards usually used in judging sports cars. Arriving in the wake of the second oil crisis, while American car engines were still adjusting to emissions and mileage standards, the DeLorean was billed as 'an ethical car'. That meant exciting performance without wasting gas, polluting the air or endangering a single

living thing. Also, the material pleasure was to be delivered at a reasonable price.

Breakdowns and repeated production problems delayed the arrival of the first DeLoreans until customer excitement had reached a buyers' frenzy in car-crazy places like Los Angeles.

There were people waiting to spend their money on an American dream they had been anticipating most of their lives. To heighten the tension, delivery of the first batch of cars in Los Angeles was kept to a small number to go on display in selected showrooms. For a week, the gleaming silver DeLorean outshone any other star in town. Eager buyers bid $10 000 and $15 000 over the sticker prices to be among the first to own the long-awaited prize. Dealers resisted the

1981 DeLorean
The gull-wings looked dramatic, but they sometimes refused to open; the glamorous shape was difficult to see out of except straight ahead; and the 'stainless steel' body showed every smudge and fingermark, making the car a rolling memorial to every person or thing that ever touched it.

offers, keeping the cars in their show windows until a larger shipment was on the way, then unloaded the first batch of cars at prices that ranged between $35 000 and $40 000 each.

By the time the second shipment of cars arrived, the grave flaw of the unpainted steel bodies was apparent. Mislabelled as stainless, the steel finish was impervious to rust and only rust, which was not a factor in California anyway. The DeLorean skin showed every smudge, every grease spot and every hand print as if the blots and marks were stencilled into the metal. Every touch left an imprint on the metal body, so the car became, instead of a mobile metal sculpture, a rolling signature of every person and thing that had touched it, like a cast autographed by hospital visitors.

Enthusiasm for the car stayed high for a matter of months. Its dirty face was overlooked as a welter of production problems surfaced for the buyers as operational problems. John Z. DeLorean assured everyone that all production problems had been solved, that early cars would be made perfect and that the cars on the way were perfect. Nothing got better. Instead, the DeLorean turned out to be a bad dream in the history of the American automobile. The car was uncomfortable, cramped and awkward inside, with miserable side and rear vision. The steering was heavy, the ride harsh and poorly modulated, the automatic transmission was unresponsive and the performance of the smog-controlled V6 was unacceptable to the average driver. The DeLorean suffered from an unreliable electrical system and chronic malfunctions in the automatic operation of the gullwing doors, which temporarily trapped once-proud owners in the prisons of their non-functioning cars.

A belated fix for the desperate body-smudge problem was announced in the form of body paint, and a twin-turbocharged high-performance DeLorean was rumoured to be on the way. But a rising tide of financial ruin swamped the company. DeLorean himself tried to keep the myth afloat until the last possible moment as the whole farce unravelled, leaving lines of unsold cars in wholesale dealers' lots waiting for buyers who were no longer interested at any price.

DeLorean's personal charisma and public relations genius was such that millions of Americans who were never subjected to the misfortune of actual contact with the car believed DeLorean had been the victim of a conspiracy of dark corporate American forces that had not wanted an independent effort to succeed. Somehow a twentieth-century hex had been placed on a noble car. DeLorean's subsequent arrest on massive charges of a cocaine-smuggling conspiracy, fraud, embezzlement and other offences, of which he was later acquitted, helped fuel the conspiracy theory.

With the DeLorean's star finally extinguished as a new American dream car, and the widening popularity of the V8 Ferrari, the V8 Mercedes-Benz and the Porsche 911, the well-heeled automotive extremist's search for something faster and more exclusive led to a new chapter in hot-rodding and customizing. The man who wanted something different, better and quicker looked to Europe for answers. They came from speciality engineering shops in Germany that did to European performance cars what California hot-rodders did to American cars in the late forties and

1987 Porsche 911 'Slopenose' and overleaf Hot-rodding took a turn upward in the 1980s, with the effort going into customizing high-buck European performance cars. Already fast to start with, the Porsche 911 and 911 Turbo became the objects of customizers who re-did the front fenders in the image of racing Porsches. The rear fenders were also widened and air-cooling ducts added; the rear spoiler too was enlarged. Instead of being a less expensive way to go faster, the Porsche 'Slopenose' conversion made an already expensive car more expensive.

fifties: they souped up the engines for more power and custom-styled the bodywork for distinctive looks under the guise of enhanced aerodynamics.

The new German high-buck hot-rods were everything the performance-oriented status-seeker could ask for. A Porsche Turbo Carrera with custom engine and bodywork by the firm B&B or the Kremer Brothers cost almost twice as much as a standard 911 Turbo Carrera. The custom-engineered Porsche had the boost pressure in the turbocharging system raised for a power increase of 40 or 50 per cent. The added power made a car which could already out-accelerate any production car in the world even quicker. The custom bodywork made a mean-looking car look meaner. Radical styling modifications copied from race cars included extra-wide rear fenders, an oversize whale-tail spoiler and a flush, streamlined nose treatment called 'slopenose', which became an underground up-market trend. By the mid-eighties, Porsches with nose jobs were familiar sights in the fast lanes and in valet parking areas in enclaves for the rich and famous from Beverly Hills to Miami.

The hot-rod Porsches had price tags to match almost anything on the road, with engine and bodywork modifications running $30 000 to $40 000 on top of a $50 000 purchase price. The German firm of AMG did

1987 Porsche 'Slopenose'

The custom Porsche profile, which was originated in the German performance speciality shops of Kremer and B & B, became an image which evolved into an underground trend. The customizing added pizzazz to a car that was exciting to begin with, making the Porsche 'Slopenose' the epitome of conspicuous consumption on wheels. Most 'Slopenose' conversions also feature modifications to increase the already stunning performance of the 911 Turbo. As with Detroit in the fifties, Porsche responded to the popularity of customized and hot-rodded 911s by offering a 'Slopenose' version from the factory, as a variation on the standard 911 or 911 Turbo. The 'Slopenose' version sells for around $100 000, compared with $40 000 to $60 000 for the standard 911. Most custom Porsche 'Slopenoses' feature custom luxury upholstery and ultra high-tech mega-watt stereo systems that cost more than the average Toyota.

similar custom body and performance tailoring on Mercedes-Benzes, turning out high-price luxury hot-rods capable of outrunning the hounds of hell without relaxing the standards of elegant, dignified motoring. Other shops did custom work on BMWs, and America was in the age of the European hot-rod.

The German hot-rods were modified in the style of racing cars, but when they reached the United States, where the speed limit was still 55 mph, they were used mainly to attract attention and make impressions. The cars were well suited to the job. The new look was called the 'Euro-style', a German version of the fifties California customizer's approach to restyling by removing chrome trim or painting it the same colour as the rest of the car. AMG Mercedes-Benzs, BMW Alpinas and Kremer Porsches showed no visible chrome trim. Even the wheels and wheel covers were painted – usually white or black – to match the body in a monocolour scheme that drew attention under the guise of pretending anonymity.

The Euro-look fad of modified Porsches, Mercedes-Benzs and BMWs turned the concept of hot-rodding and customizing 180 degrees from its starting point.

spread to the lowest-priced German range, and from them to mid-priced and low-priced Japanese and American cars. Side spoilers and monochrome paint schemes became a new fashion trend for people who were unconcerned with performance but obsessed with style.

And as the Euro-look German hot-rods spread, there were some who went farther, especially in California where extremism is practised as a lifestyle. In the sunshine state where hot-rodding was born, a handful of radical performance-seekers were driving out-and-out racing cars on deserted freeways in the early morning hours before dawn. Centred in or near Los Angeles, these men owned Lola and McLaren race cars made for the 24 Hours of Le Mans or the 24 Hours of Daytona and used them for illegal adventures at light aircraft speeds. These were the ultimate in esoteric, elitist image cars, knee-high coupes made by companies the average sports car enthusiast did not even know about. The underground nickname 'Banzai Runner' was given to these 180 mph driving fanatics, and the term entered the lexicon of status performance cars. Tales of 'Banzai Runners' in 190 mph or 200 mph

1970 McLaren M8D
During the 1970s, a radical new expression of hot-rodding emerged in the fast-car underground of Los Angeles, where a tiny clique of performance extremists made solitary top-speed runs on the freeways in the small hours of the morning. Driving racing cars like this McLaren Canadian-American challenge racing car, these outlaw freeway runners got the name 'Banzai Runners'. They piloted their costly cars at up to 200 mph on near deserted highways, their cars too fast and their appearances too brief to run any risk of being caught by the law.

Instead of the resourcefulness of garage mechanics making cheap cars go faster and look better than luxury cars, this was rich guys paying auto entrepreneurs to make their expensive cars even more expensive than the next guy's expensive car. The Euro-look Mercedes-Benz and BMW fitted perfectly with the pastels and muted chroma of the popular TV show *Miami Vice*, where they became the image car of the new class of criminal multi-millionaires of the narcotics trade. The rising popularity of the Euro-look as a styling concept spawned imitations from custom shops right across the United States. From the top-line Porsche, BMW and Mercedes-Benz models, the styling

racing cars setting up unwitting drivers of 170 mph Ferraris and Porsches in money races added to the growing lore of street-hustling legend that dated back to hot-rodding in the early fifties and probably even before that.

Ferraris were souped-up and customized, too. Though it would have seemed an unthinkable insult to a thoroughbred performance car in the fifties or sixties, Berlinetta Boxers were turbocharged for greater speed, fenders flared for a wider stance and displayed in southern California showrooms as $100 000 cars good for 190 mph or more. Most of the speed claims were flagrant exaggerations for cars that seldom

reached 180 mph in the rare perfomance tests. But it was image once again, with the status of the speed claim and the price more important than the proof. The wheel had turned full circle: as had been true in the twenties and early thirties, ultimate performance and all-out speed were reserved for the very rich. Even at the actual speeds realized in performance tests, the high-dollar Euro hot-rods of the eighties were much, much faster than anything within the reach of the traditional American hot-rod approach to Chevys, Mustangs, Trans-Ams and Corvettes.

But American cars had not been standing still. The American V8 had ignored the widespread obituaries

1987 Mercedes-Benz 320 E AMG
The monochrome 'Euro-look' by the Stuttgart firm AMG, with body, chrome trim and wheel rims painted the same colour, became popular in Los Angeles, Miami and other American cities as the ultimate statement in a Mercedes-Benz. The AMG styling complements engine and suspension modifications for improved performance.

that were repeatedly delivered during the late seventies, declaring it an obsolete technology from a bygone era. Typed as a profligate with wasteful fuel habits and an inherently unsanitary exhaust, the V8 was no longer seen as justifiable in an age of new priorities. Cars were smaller and would get even smaller still; V8s would not be needed. Four cylinders would be plenty for most cars, with the V6 available to indulge those who insisted on having more than enough.

But the predictions assumed that oil prices would continue to rise until gasoline pump prices reached the $2.50 or $3.00 a gallon found in Europe. Instead, the wave of oil price inflation crested in 1979 and prices

189

actually fell back in the eighties. By 1982, gasoline pump prices had dropped down to under $1.00 a gallon, which no longer seemed high. The price was actually four times what it had been twenty years before, a rise no higher than general inflation.

Chrysler, however, had sidelined the V8 performance engine, focusing development on basic four-cylinder engines, with a turbocharged four for added power. Though it was often rumoured that GM was on the verge of dropping the V8 in favour of the V6, the eight-cylinder American standby remained in production, even though the V6 was pegged as the engine of the future. Ford hedged its bets with a turbocharged four-

1985 Ford Mustang SVO
Showing a distinctly European influence, the SVO Mustang featured a double rear spoiler, special shock absorbers and suspension and a turbocharged four-cylinder motor. Though quick and responsive, the SVO Mustang failed to keep up with the sales of the V8 Mustang GT.

cylinder engine for performance versions of the Mustang, with its V6 and trusty V8 available as options. In addition major advances in computer-programmed electronic fuel management finally brought the V8 into compliance with emission regulations and delivered more power from less fuel than engines of ten or twenty years earlier.

In 1982, Ford had a performance V8 on the line that was smoother, more powerful and more responsive than performance engines of the sixties. It came in the fourth-generation Ford Mustang. Introduced in 1978, the Mustang was stylistically unexciting—wedge-shaped with reverse angles and flat planes. But for 1982 the styling faded to secondary importance in the excitement over the born-again V8. The new HO (High Output) engine option suddenly made Mustang the fastest-accelerating American production car. All the old virtues that had made American cars so satisfying in the fifties and sixties were prominent in the Ford V8 for 1982. The fuel-injection system was perfectly in tune with the electronically regulated spark, the unleaded fuel and the smoothly integrated emissions equipment. After years of suffering unpleasant V8s that alternately surged and coughed at low speeds, bogged down at full throttle and ran out of breath at high rpms, the American performance enthusiast was delighted with an engine from Ford that had a smooth, iron-fisted power delivery of solid muscle from the bottom of the rev range to the redline.

The 1982 Mustang HO was a harsh-riding car that achieved road-holding at the expense of comfort. The unsophisticated solid rear-axle suspension could not deliver smooth ride and at the same time good high-speed handling, so ride comfort was sacrificed. In a car capable of 127 mph in third gear, a tough ride could be forgiven, and the Mustang was a strong success in the

1982 Chevrolet Camaro Z28

General Motors moved back into design leadership with the all-new Camaro and Firebird for 1982. The Camaro shared body shell and design with the Pontiac Firebird, one of the most successful shapes in American automotive history. A sophisticated suspension gave the Z28 superior handling, although the engines offered in the first two years were short on power. Chevrolet corrected this with a 305 cubic-inch tuned-port injection V8, then offered the sizzling 350 cubic-inch Corvette engine with tuned-port injection.

market, bringing performance lustre back to the Ford name again.

In 1982 Chevrolet and Pontiac introduced a new Camaro/Firebird with all-new sheet-metal over a lightened, shortened, re-engineered car that immediately put GM on an equal footing in styling with any designers in Europe. The new Camaro and Firebird were stunning cars. They looked modern and fresh in an age of styling which seemed dictated by computer programmes dedicated to efficiency in search of high mileage. Though the Camaro/Firebird was aerodynamically efficient, the clean airflow was achieved with sensuous curves and sweeping contours in an elegant, flawless execution of line that left nothing for the customizer or after-market specialist to improve.

This held true except for under the hood. The Camaro and Firebird were disappointing in action, with performance that fell far short of the exciting styling. The V8 offered in both cars was rated on paper as equal in output to the Mustang HO engine, but the heavier GM pony cars were decisively slower than the Mustang. Neither the Camaro nor the Firebird compared to the Mustang HO in acceleration or top speed.

GM promised an improved powerplant soon, and made good the promise.

Just as the Mustang represented the rebirth of the American V8, the new Camaro/Firebird embodied all the native American glamour and design beauty of the best of the fifties and sixties car styles. Though the Camaro/Firebird was unmistakably modern, it was not drawn in the European image. It had as much flow and harmony of line as the Ferrari 308GTB without being derivative. It was a triumph of all-American styling that suddenly brought the pony car up to date in handling.

1987 Ford Thunderbird Turbo Coupe
A fresh, European-accented design that caught on quickly with American buyers, the Thunderbird Turbo Coupe was a performance-oriented car in the spirit of the classic 1955–7 T-Bird two-seaters.

The Camaro Z28 and the Firebird Trans-Am were rated among the best-handling cars ever tested by American enthusiast magazines, and the skid pad numbers were among the highest ever recorded for production cars, including Ferrari and Porsche.

It was ironic that GM's beauties were handicapped by weak engines, the area dominated by Chevrolet and Pontiac since 1955. But the cars sold initially on looks alone, even without the engine they deserved. A year later, a more powerful performance engine option was offered with significantly increased horsepower,

which put the Camaro on an equal footing with the Mustang GT.

Pontiac had introduced a mid-engined two-seater called the Fiero that was either sports car or economy car, depending on which GM ad you read. It looked like a sports car, but it was powered by an iron four-cylinder engine that gave distinctly economy-car performance. The Fiero styling was well received by the public and so was the car, even though it shared the Camaro/Firebird's lack of a proper engine. A fix for the Fiero was said to be on the way in the form of a V6, but it would be slow in arriving.

Meanwhile, Ford introduced a completely revised Thunderbird called the Turbo Coupe. Two decades of weight gains and styling degeneration had hardened the Thunderbird's arteries and turned it into a bloated, middle-of-the-road luxury car with mediocre styling, lacklustre performance and unwieldy size. Suddenly it was back to the classic two-seater image of the fifties with a sleek, compact, two-door sports coupe that was stylish and flowing where the Mustang was sharp-edged and angular. The Thunderbird suspension was more advanced than the Mustang but it, too, was handicapped by a four-cylinder engine when it deserved an eight. The turbocharged four put out as much or more net horsepower than the V8, but lacked the V8 smoothness which a buyer in this price class expected. The turbo-four also lacked the bigger engine's low-speed torque.

Nevertheless, the Thunderbird Turbo Coupe was a success in the triumph of a European-style performance motor over the traditional American V8. Americans had demonstrated that, whether other things were equal or not, they preferred V8s in cars with any sort of macho performance image. But the Turbo Thunder-bird was such a slick, sleek package that it succeeded anyway, despite its four-cylinder engine.

The Thunderbird Turbo Coupe was, however, no longer the only car for its marketing niche. It was in a field of increasingly tough competition from Japanese sports cars that were moving in on different price levels. Mazda had the budget-priced rotary-engined RX-7 sports car at a Mustang price and the faster RX-7 Turbo a notch above Ford's Thunderbird Turbo Coupe. Toyota's new Supra sports car also came both naturally aspirated and turbocharged, as did Nissan's 300ZX.

Turbocharging was a new performance feature that was spreading down the price levels of Japanese sports compacts, along with the double-overhead-camshaft engine, which was a big performance jump ahead of

1987 Mazda RX-7 Elford
Rotary-engined with a high power output for its size, the Mazda RX-7 helped redefine the sports car in the American market. Quick, comfortable, manoeuvrable, attractively styled and affordably priced, the RX-7 was an immediate hit in the US.

the single-overhead-cam engine that had been an innovation a dozen years earlier. Along with double-overhead cams, Japanese and German auto-makers were offering cylinder heads with four valves per cylinder instead of two. The quad-valve engine was another spillover of racing-engine development to production-car engines in the increasingly stiff international market competition that was becoming an out-and-out technology race.

In 1983, Chevrolet introduced an all-new Corvette, the first genuinely new Corvette since 1968. The old Mako Shark Corvette had been long overdue for retirement when the new Corvette arrived. Styling

1988 Chevrolet Corvette

The convertible Corvette for the 1980s was introduced in 1983 with a new body covering an all-new car. Replacing the ageing Stingray which had been in continuous production with few significant changes since 1968, the new Corvette was a milestone in American automotive history. Gone was the cramped cockpit, the punishing stiff ride, the poor accommodations and the mediocre performance that had reduced the Corvette to a pale caricature of itself. The new Corvette features state-of-the-art front and rear suspension for cornering power previously found only on racing cars. The 350 cubic-inch tuned-port injection provides stunning acceleration and exhilarating top speed.

that had been exciting in 1968 was long since outdated by 1980, and the Corvette seemed to be skating by on borrowed time in the last years before the new car. The cramped, incommodious interior with inadequate passenger or luggage space and the rough, punishing ride hurt the Corvette image compared to Japanese cars such as the 300ZX, the Supra and the RX-7 Turbo, which showed up the Corvette's weaknesses. Corvette performance with the 350 cubic-inch engine, the largest Chevrolet passenger car engine in production, was no longer a bottom line pay-off that excused other shortcomings. By 1981, Corvette performance had reached a low-water mark, the result of continuous weight gain and power loss to government regulations.

Everything changed in 1983 with the introduction of the new Corvette, which evoked the same level of excitement that had greeted the Sting Ray in 1963. The 1984 Corvette, given an early introduction in 1983,

1988 Chevrolet Corvette
The new Corvette finally fulfilled the promise that had lain fallow during the seventies, putting Corvette back on an equal footing with Porsche and giving it performance superiority over the V8 Ferrari 308GTB.

delivered everything that American enthusiasts had been wanting from Chevrolet for years. Like the special 1963-6 Sting Ray, the 1984 Corvette was a superbly balanced, well-integrated machine incorporating advanced performance and handling technology in a glamorous, stylish package. The 1984 Corvette had almost perfect fore-and-aft weight balance for neutral handling, thanks to a rear-set engine and suspension parts and running gear made of forged aluminium, magnesium and plastic.

Though the ride of the new Corvette was initially faulted for being too stiff, the glaring weaknesses of poor directional stability and inaccurate tracking of the old Corvette were gone. So was the cramped interior. The new Corvette was everything the old Corvette was not. It was spacious inside, with compact exterior dimensions. Instead of wasting space with an extravagantly shaped body, the new Corvette was a model of interior space efficiency. Ride comfort aside, the new Corvette offered skid pad and racetrack handling levels that was superior to any current production car. The Chevy V8 with tuned-port injection gave the new Corvette acceleration on a par with that of the bigger-block versions of the early seventies and a higher top speed as well.

The new Corvette styling was eye-catching and arrestingly good-looking without being the triumph achieved by the Camaro and the Trans-Am. Stunning in red, yellow or black, the new Corvette was merely handsome in the popular eighties earth-tones of beige, gold and tan. But the performance and the new level of sophisticated road-holding put the Corvette in a place it had never been before: in the top rank of world-class performance sports cars, with the Porsche 911 Carrera, the 928S and 944 Turbo. The Corvette could easily outperform the Ferrari 308GTsi at less than half the price. It was a proud day for the American enthusiast to see America's all-time favourite sports car reborn in fulfilment of the promise that had gone undelivered for so long.

With the Z51 performance-option package, the 1984 Corvette was once again the fastest American production car, with a 0-to-60 time of six seconds and a top speed touching 150 mph. Though not as fierce in acceleration as the fastest 427 Corvettes of the sixties, it was a vastly more comfortable and practical on the street and it was quicker around a race track than those big-engined monsters. The new Corvette was close to a racing car at birth. It almost immediately

proved itself, racing in a new series of sports car racing called Showroom Stock for cars to be raced in basically unmodified form. The Corvette quickly became a leading contender in this class, with serious competition only from the Porsche 944 Turbo. Improvements generated from racetrack experience were funnelled

1988 Chevrolet Corvette
The reborn Corvette cockpit features spage-age digital displays which are not to everyone's taste. But the performance includes a 150 mph top speed and a 0-to-60 time of six seconds, which makes the Corvette one of the fastest cars sold in America. A sophisticated suspension and a spacious, plush interior packages blazing muscle-car performance in a personal luxury-car format. With styling to remain basically unchanged during a projected run of several years, the new Corvette returned topless-style motoring to high performance. The standard Corvette comes with removable panel tops; the stunningly handsome convertible is more popular and more expensive.

1982 Chevrolet 4 × 4 Pickup

A rage for rugged, heavy metal full-size trucks was part of the cultural wave that brought macho back in style for the eighties. Like Sylvester Stallone and Arnold Schwarzenegger, the four-wheel-drive trucks from Chevy, Ford and Dodge were muscle on top of muscle, with every bulge on display. Overcab light bars and oversize wheels and tyres completed the image of automotive menace for a huge number of American asphalt cowboys who believe in Hank Williams Jr, Rocky, Rambo and the right to beer and bear arms.

back to the factory and into the production line for continual refinement of the street car.

Fast as it was, the Corvette was still inferior to Porsche in acceleration and top speed, coming in second to the 911 Carrera, the Turbo Carrera, the 928S and the 944 Turbo. But, amazingly for Chevrolet, the Z51-optioned Corvette recorded higher skid pad test figures, and turned marginally quicker times at the race track. Once again it was a predator on the loose. Considering that the faster Porsches cost twice as much and the Ferrari almost three times the Corvette's $23 000 price, GM had finally done justice to Corvette's role as America's dream car.

The comeback of the American performance car coincided with the rising popularity of the pick-up truck as the urban cowboy spirit spread through America. The Wild West was alive in off-road racing, the rough, ragged and dangerous sport played in Baja California, the harsh Mexican peninsula, where the last frontier might be challenged in competition. The rough-tough Baja off-road look of raised-body pick-ups with side stripes and oversize tyres, bumper bars, overhead roll bars and driving lights spread from Baja racing dune-buggies and single-purpose racers to become a new image for the street, a new kind of automotive lifestyle. It brought a fresh styling wave for maxi-pick-ups,

mini-pick-ups, jeeps and the four-wheel-drive Chevy Blazer and Ford Bronco that had added a popular new shape to the truck-jeep hybrid field, a rapidly expanding new market segment.

The eighties were a growth period in jeep popularity. The currents of Baja and truck-love, as well as a natural fondness for the jeep, converged to make it a major vehicle in American car culture. The jeep had experienced a style revival on its own in the late seventies, as its popularity with desert recreational drivers, off-road racers and jeep-lovers produced yet another California cult car. This underground trend grew into what became jeep chic. The rugged, funky, Western lines of the hunky, high-bodied jeep somehow looked just right on Melrose Avenue in Hollywood or Brattle Street in Cambridge, Massachusetts, or on the beach in the Hamptons on Long Island. The jeep's

military background and indomitable reputation from off-road use contributed to an image tailor-made for a new fashion wave that adopted LL Bean fishing, hunting and camping gear along with Perrier water and Rebok running shoes.

American Motors, which had failed in almost every effort at pleasing the American public with a car, finally succeeded in the high-tech, fashion-conscious New Age of the eighties with a forty-year-old military-utility vehicle that had been designed originally to replace the horse in the Army in the late thirties. Though the jeep was totally unsuited for wet weather and was uncomfortable and unsatisfactory in the cold, it was made for sunny southern California. The jeep was a perfect vehicle to go cruising down the malls on shopping safaris; and as a vehicle to be seen in it was ideal, since it had almost no body.

1985 Jeep CJ7
Built by American Motors in the image of the military vehicle used extensively in World War II, the jeep was an unlikely popular success in the 1980s. First popularized by off-roaders and desert trekkers, the jeep became a popular urban shopping safari vehicle. Midway between a truck and a sports car, the jeep had a unique personality that attracted loyal followers right across the country.

1980 BMW 633

Seemingly without the notice of General Motors, Cadillac was unseated as the most desired luxury car in the 1970s. By 1980, there was no question that Mercedes-Benz was the most desired status car in the US, with BMW running a close second. The Yuppie Baby-boom generation, which was identified as the crucial market sector, showed a clear preference for European prestige cars over American sedans. BMW's four-cylinder 3-Series sedan was the most affordable. The 633 sports coupe, powered by an overhead-camshaft six, shared top status honours for BMW with the luxury 733 sedan. Though not a sports car in the sense of a Porsche, Ferrari or Corvette, the 633 coupe became a strong prestige car for its sleek, graceful lines and general monied aura, more than making up for the slightly weak performance.

While the Corvette brought performance prestige back to General Motors, the Cadillac image continued to falter and BMW and Mercedes-Benz lengthened their lead as prestige image cars with people under fifty. Though Cadillac sales continued slowly to expand, and the total was many times the sum of Mercedes-Benz and BMW sales combined, the Cadillac buyers were predominantly older Americans who had grown up believing Cadillac was the best and had not changed their outlook.

Among younger professionals and the college-educated 'opinion-leaders', whom all the auto companies sought as customers, Cadillac had lost its image as a status car or even a high-quality automobile. Instead, Mercedes-Benz, BMW, Volvo, Audi and Saab were seen as prestige cars in terms of engineering and performance quality as well as status.

The problem was obvious from Cadillac styling, which was hopelessly off the mark. Though the ornate, high-roof, chop-back style called 'Opera Roof' was considered elegant through the mid-West and by retirement-age folks across the country, it was as outdated to most younger Americans as a polyester leisure suit.

The problem went much deeper than styling for Cadillac, which needed appeal in young age groups when its loyal buyers were taken away by old age. While the German and Swedish cars favoured by the Yuppie buyer did not necessarily shine in styling, they were known for engineering and technological sophistication, an image that was crucial for young Americans in the eighties. The automotive engineering values of the Perrier generation were multi-valve, overhead-camshaft engine technology, independent suspension and four-wheel disc anti-skid braking systems. Not because the Yuppies understood what they were, but because they were advertised and featured by the cars they knew were the best: Saab, Volvo, Audi, BMW and Mercedes-Benz.

The Seville, Cadillac's mid-sized answer to Mercedes and BMW for the seventies, completely lacked the engineering appeal of the cars it was produced to compete with. Though Cadillac made a token, belated effort at 'European-style' cars, the traditional Cadillac buyer was not interested and the customers Cadillac wanted were not fooled. Unlike other GM divisions which had engineered exciting performance out of the V8, Cadillac had long since dropped completely out of the performance picture. The $30 000 Cadillac de Ville of 1984 could be out-accelerated and outrun by

1983 Saab Turbo
The Yuppie, for Young, Upwardly-mobile Professional, favoured almost anything European over American cars. Saab was one of the most desired cars for the Baby-boomers, who liked it in spite of, or perhaps because of, its rather odd styling. From an eccentric, slightly weird Scandinavian car with a crackling three-cylinder engine in the fifties and sixties, Saab evolved into an upscale, high-dollar prestige performance car. Saab is seen as an eminently respectable car with an image of good value, rugged dependability and high-quality engineering.

almost any $9000 Japanese import. It was a long way down from the Cadillac of earlier decades which had worn its prestige title as the best performance car on the road. From the car with the most advanced American technology in the fifties, Cadillac had merely kept pace through the sixties and then appeared to have lost all interest in technological progress in the seventies, perhaps in the belief that its customers were too old to notice. The ill-advised and unsuccessful Cadillac diesel and the bizarre, multi-phase V8 with alternate firing modes from eight to six to four cylinders

1983 Saab Turbo
If there had been no Saab Turbos, as much a symbol of America in the eighties as Hagen-Daaz ice cream, aerobics, Rebok high-tops, Madonna and Sean Penn, Yuppies would have been limited to Audi, Volvo, BMW and Mercedes-Benz for automotive choices.

depending on engine load had not helped the car in marketplace competition against the real engineering advances made by Mercedes-Benz, BMW, Volvo, Saab and Audi.

Chrysler had taken a similar route by sidelining the V8, the traditional symbol of the luxury car, to compete in the prestige-car market with an economy-car platform powered by a four-cylinder economy-car engine. A reborn luxury image for Chrysler would have to wait for a new car born of new technology, which would be a long time in coming.

Lincoln, however, re-emerged as a surprise prestige-car in the eighties with a new edition of the Continental called the Mark VII. Built on the same chassis platform and sharing sheet-metal with the classy new Thunderbird, the Continental MK VII gracefully retired the awkward, overstyled, overweight and overwrought Mark VI in a return to the look of the svelte, elegant Continental MK II of the fifties. The MK VII had the sweeping flow and broad-shouldered, wide-hipped appeal of American luxury cars of the fifties and early sixties brought up to date for the eighties. The Continental MK VII harked back to the days of the American luxury car as a smooth-riding style-setter with satisfying performance from a powerful engine and with advanced engineering appropriate to its station.

The MK VII won immediate praise for its styling, which was modern without any hint of the prevailing wedge shapes or angles. Instead it had a contoured, sculpted mass that appeared both low and wide, with considerable heft, and a high belt-line. The MK VII had the expected plushness inside with deep leather seats and trim, without the luxury motel-suite decor favoured by Cadillac and Chrysler, and by Lincoln for its larger, old-fashioned Town Car.

The MK VII featured a complex air-suspension design utilizing computer-controlled air bags instead of springs for a continually variable ride compliance designed to provide the best of handling and comfort without compromising either. It offered computer-controlled anti-lock braking to complement the suspension for a responsive, controllable, driver's car – a package containing the qualities Yuppies sought in European cars. The MK VII broke the tradition of Lincoln luxury-car image which had followed the Cadillac mould of the big, soft-riding American boat with every styling gimmick and luxury convenience added for good measure.

Ford, however, doubted the demand for a real driver's vehicle like the MK VII, so the car was offered in two versions: a 'Designer' edition styled by Bill Blass, Versace or Giannini, and an LSC version without the fake wire-wheel discs, body stripes and designer interior. The LSC outsold the Designer edition four-to-one, appealing to an older enthusiast buyer who appreciated power, prestige, good looks and modern engineering in an American car. The performance V8 from the hot Mustang was first made optional, then standard equipment in response to popular demand. With the 200hp engine, the Lincoln MK VII was an excellent example of a car particularly dear to Americans: a big, heavy,

1984 Lincoln Continental MK VII
One of the few American luxury cars to catch the American fancy in the eighties, the MK VII brought high performance back to Lincoln. The most popular version of the MK VII is the high-performance LSC, powered by the 225hp V8 shared with the Mustang GT. The MK VII features electronically controlled air suspension and anti-lock disc brakes, a plush interior, a smooth ride and a pleasing, luxurious shape. The MK VII shares a body/chassis platform with the Thunderbird and continues the tradition of a rear-drive V8 while other Ford family cars moved to the more modern configuration of front-wheel drive.

good-looking high-speed highway cruiser with the handling and suspension refinement to take a good road fast, with a powerful V8 under the hood. The LSC with the HO engine option reminded auto-magazine writers of the 1960 pop record *Hot Rod Lincoln*, which told of a street race between a Ford hot-rod with a Lincoln engine and a Cadillac. As in all the other American hot-rod racing songs, the hot-rod won.

The hot-rod Lincoln was so popular that owners wanted a look the factory did not provide – the Euro-hotrod look in AMG black-on-black or white-on-

1984 Lincoln Continental MK VII

The sumptuous interior of the Lincoln was American indulgence at its best with tucked and pleated deep-cushioned seats and electronic adjustments for every conceivable position, the MK VII package combined old-fashioned American big-car plush with modern road-holding.

white, *Miami Vice* style. After-market custom specialists created their own all-black or all-white 'Euro-style' MK VIIs, and some shops offered performance modifications as well. The custom hot-rod Lincoln was an expensive car, with the 'AMG' style treatment adding between $7000 and $10 000 to the $22 000 price. It was cheap to the buyer, however, considering the price of a Mercedes 300E or BMW 528 or a Jaguar XJ-S, and more desirable to the man over forty who still remembered the hot-rod era of the early fifties and preferred an American car.

THE LATE EIGHTIES

The return of performance and style in a Detroit resurgence

The sensuous new Chevy Camaro and Pontiac Firebird moved American auto style back in the forefront, with a high-performance Chevy V8 on the boil again. The Camaro IROC Z and the Mustang GT put Ford and Chevy on performance parity with the Porsche 944 and the Ferrari 308GTS. Buick clawed its way to the top of the American performance peak with the snarling, tyre-smoking Regal Grand National – a turbocharged, V6-powered smoker as fast as the fastest sixties muscle cars. All previous eras of car cult were replayed. Hot-rods and customs from earlier decades returned and hot-rodding took a new direction as upscale status-seekers customized Porsche Turbo Carreras, Mercedes-Benzes, Ferrari Testarossas and BMWs.

FOR 1985, GM upgraded the Chevy V8 to make an honest car out of the Camaro, which badly needed more power to live up to its looks and keep pace with the lighter, cheaper and faster Mustang. Ford had taken the performance lead over Chevrolet in 1982 with the 157hp high-output version of the 302 cubic-inch V8, which made the Mustang quicker than the heavier 165hp Camaro. In 1983 the Mustang HO rating was raised to 175hp and late in 1984 a 205hp version was available. For 1985, Ford continued the escalation with a 210hp engine.

It was not easy for Chevrolet to catch up. The simple hot-rodding tricks that had raised power output so many times through the fifties and sixties would no longer work. Everything that could be done with old methods had already been done. The complex web of ever-tightening emissions and mileage standards made traditional hot-rodding techniques obsolete, and the only legal route to more power was new technology. In the past, major performance advances had come from the independent innovation of self-taught hot-rodders and speed-tuners in small garages and back-alley shops. By 1985, computer programming was integral to engine performance research and horse-power gains were likely to come from abroad.

To get more street power from the small-block V8, Chevrolet used a fuel-injection system developed by Bosch of Germany for Porsche 962 racing cars and adapted to the Porsche 928 V8 sports car. Fuel injection was not new to Chevrolet, but the system adopted for the 1985 engines was. It replaced the unsuccessful throttle-body system which Chevrolet called 'cross-fire' injection on both Corvette and Camaro engines. For 1985, Chevy went to the more complex and more expensive port-injection system in which the fuel-air mix was squirted directly into each cylinder by an individual injector port. The port-injection system developed for the Camaro and Corvette engines used long, tuned runners to each cylinder for a ram-charge effect to the fuel-air mix which greatly enhanced mid-range torque and improved overall power output.

The heart of the tuned-port injection system was the Bosch 'hotwire' airflow sensor for each runner that metered fuel delivery through a computer-programmed control module. The use of Porsche racing-engine tech-nology in a Chevrolet street car pointed up how

1987 Camaro IROC Z
Pressed by the hard-charging Ford Mustang GT, Chevrolet introduced the IROC Z version of the Camaro Z28. The 1987 model offered a choice of engines including two different tuned-port injection V8s that made the IROC Z one of the strongest performers on the road. The maturing of computer-programmed electronic fuel and airflow management put Chevrolet back on the leading edge of V8 performance for the eighties. Though priced at almost $20 000 fully equipped with the tuned-port injection V8, the IROC Z offers strong performance car value.

narrow the performance parameters for cars had become. Without space-age racing technology under the hood, the power, smoothness and performance Americans expected was not available with the fuel economy and clean exhaust government standards required. The competition to improve performance within the bounds of government regulations had taken on the complex crisis atmosphere of racing engine development.

That made it doubly appropriate for Chevy to name the hottest 1985 Camaro with tuned-port injection the 'IROC Z', after the International Race of Champions (IROC for short), a televised racing series watched by millions. It featured a field of top drivers in identical racing-prepared Camaro Z28s competing for a large cash purse at major American tracks. But even with the IROC name and tuned-port injection, the 1985 305 Camaro was a notch behind Mustang in speed. So for 1986, Chevrolet stepped up to the 350 cubic-inch tuned-port injection Corvette engine, which delivered

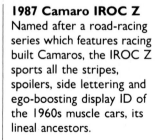

220hp in the Camaro and finally gave Chevy performance parity with Ford.

Development on the Mustang engine had not been standing still, and the GT engine had received an even more sophisticated fuel-injection system called sequential port injection that raised the Mustang power output to 225hp by 1987. But the greater torque from the bigger Chevy engine more than made up for the difference in horsepower and put Chevrolet back on the performance front with one of the fastest production cars on the road.

While the power figures look modest next to the awesome numbers claimed for sixties muscle cars,

1987 Camaro IROC Z
Named after a road-racing series which features racing built Camaros, the IROC Z sports all the stripes, spoilers, side lettering and ego-boosting display ID of the 1960s muscle cars, its lineal ancestors.

the late eighties Corvette, Mustang and Camaro went faster with comparable weights and less rated horsepower than their fabled sixties ancestors. The discrepancy in claimed horsepower comes from the change in 1973 from gross to net power ratings, which substantially lowered the figure, putting it much closer to a real-world number. So an equivalent in 1965 horses to a 1986 220hp engine would be over 400hp.

The Corvette motor made the Camaro IROC Z a smoking gun, a street-fighter looking for trouble. But, like the famous sixties muscle cars, the Corvette-engined IROC Z was a no-compromise performance vehicle which skimped on comfort for all-out acceleration.

The more civilized 5-litre version, which was raised to 215hp for 1987 and almost as fast, was far more practical for ordinary driving. With either engine, both of which were also available in the nearly identical Pontiac Firebird, the GM pony car was not only the best-looking, but one of the fastest and best-handling American sedans ever built.

With anti-roll bars front and rear, high-compliance suspension and Goodyear Eagle radials on wide alloy wheels, the IROC Z and Mustang GT raised American sedan performance to an all-time high, with true racetrack handling to match the acceleration and speed. The IROC Z had superior braking capacity, with four-

1987 Camaro IROC Z
With its superb road-holding, excellent brakes and brilliant acceleration, the IROC Z combines high levels of performance with flawless styling. The latest generation Camaro brings the American performance sedan into the front line of road sports cars for the eighties.

wheel discs compared to the Mustang's rear drums, and slightly more comfort at speed. Both cars used the same high-performance rubber: super-low profile Goodyear Eagle VRs rated for over 130 mph.

A 1987 test by *Car & Driver* magazine clocked the Mustang GT at 137 mph in fifth gear, with a 0-to-60 time of 6.3 seconds, compared to a 7 second 0-to-60 time and 135 mph top speed for the 5-litre IROC Z. The Corvette-engined Camaro was not tested because the magazine staff felt the car's comfort level was unsatisfactorily compromised by the ultimate engine option. The two smaller-engined cars, though, IROC Z and Mustang GT, delivered speed with a sophistication

extraordinary for two American sedans that had been born and raised as economy family vehicles.

While the IROC Z stickered at close to $20 000 with the Corvette engine, the Mustang GT was an extraordinary buy at under $14 000. But the prices still kept both cars out of the hands of most teenagers until they were used or stolen – which happened frequently. The cars were so desirable to people who could not afford them that a high theft rate made them extremely expensive to insure, with liability premiums that reflected the frequency of theft and crashes from overenthusiastic driving.

The Camaro and Mustang, like all the other V8-powered rear-drive cars in both lines, were designs living on borrowed time, at least according to people who saw lightweight front-wheel-drive compacts as the technology of the nineties. GM was busy producing front-wheel-drive cars in the Euro/Oriental image such as the V6-powered Pontiac Bonneville SE, and Ford stepped square into future technology with the European-styled, front-wheel-drive Taurus/Sable, an innovative, imaginative car that got the market success it deserved.

But the real performance excitement stayed with technology of the past in the V8-powered rear-drivers. This left Chrysler out of the dream-car business of

1987 Buick Grand National
Sharing a chassis platform with the conservatively luxurious Regal, the Grand National is a smoking, clawing exercise in the adventure of performance excess. With more power on tap than called for in any legal situation, the Grand National jolted the staid Buick image and became an instant collector's item.

the eighties. Having sidelined the V8 and rear-drive configuration for performance passenger cars, Chrysler used a four-cylinder economy engine to power a performance car, a front-drive compact developed from the K-car platform. The turbocharged front-wheel-drive Daytona Z fastback coupe was a fast car that got even faster when modified by Carroll Shelby as a Shelby Daytona Z. The Shelby version was Chrysler president Lee Iacocca's attempt to recreate the magic chemistry of the Shelby Mustang to glamorize the Chrysler image. The limited-production Shelby Daytona Z featured a turbocharger with intercooling, another example of racing technology used to extract more power from a street engine. The intercooler was a radiator for the fuel-air mix that cooled it for greater density before combustion. The intercooled, turbo-charged Daytona Z delivered tyre-smoking performance in the Shelby tradition with appropriately modified suspension, brakes and body styling. The Shelby Z delivered sensational performance for its engine size, with racetrack laps, acceleration times and top speeds rivalling or beating the Camaro and Mustang. But in spite of the impressive performance technology, the four-cylinder, K-car based Dodge did not have the appeal of the V8 Chevy and Mustang. It was a matter of passion, not performance numbers. The American love affair with the V8 was still on.

In a surprising move, considering its staid image, Buick stirred up tremendous performance excitement by building a turbocharged V6 that out-performed all the V8s on the market. The hot Buick was the Regal Grand National, a street racer with truly savage performance in a body styled after the Buick NASCAR racing stock car. The NASCAR Buick Regal, of course, was a Buick only in name and basic body shape. Like all stock-car racers, the car was fabricated entirely from special racing parts except for the engine, a few pieces of sheet metal and the family name. The production Regal Grand National engine was a variation on the racing turbocharged V6 that put Buick-powered racing cars on the grid at the Indianapolis 500. Performance-lovers in the Buick division put the turbo V6 into a street car that lived up to the racetrack name.

An old-fashioned, large-size, rear-drive hot-rod in an era dedicated to the development of down-size European-oriented front-wheel-drive cars, the Regal Grand National was an evolutionary sidetrack for Buick and GM. It was an automotive counterpart to the bulging pectorals and biceps that helped Sylvester Stallone and Arnold Schwarzenegger outsell other action

film stars of the late eighties, in an unexpected comeback of muscle and macho after both had been pronounced passé. Like Schwarzenegger and Stallone, the Grand National was muscle on top of muscle in a body that had been around for years, with brainpower a distant second to strength. The car had a big-hipped, broad-shouldered stance on fat tyres with wide rims. Trim was black instead of chrome with tinted glass for a thoroughly menacing appearance that promised all speed and no foreplay, which is what the Grand National delivered.

The Grand National V6 was an intercooled, turbo-charged tornado conservatively rated by Buick at

1988 Buick Grand National and overleaf Powered by a turbocharged V6, the Grand National was the hottest accelerating car for sale in the US in 1988. All muscle and no brains, just a hot engine in a dated, rear-drive chassis, the GN delivers one of the most exciting rides on wheels.

245hp – more than any other American production engine. There is reason to believe the horsepower figure was deliberately understated in deference to the more conservative elements in GM management, who were probably uncomfortable with a wild Buick street racer in the first place.

Whatever the true power output may have been, the Buick Grand National was one of the fastest accelerating cars ever sold in America at any price, period. The 4.6 second 0-to-60 time recorded by *Car & Driver* in 1987 beats even the mighty Cobra 427, not to mention the 435 hp Corvette 427, the Dodge hemi-Charger, 440 Magnum and other big-block legends of the sixties. It

made the Grand National faster off the line than almost every production car in the world, including the Lamborghini Countach and the Ferrari Testarossa. A hotter and even faster Grand National for 1987 was available in a special, limited edition of 500 called the GNX, with an engine worked up to 300hp. The GNXs were instant performance legends which Buick dealers held off the market and hoarded until they could command huge mark-ups over the suggested sticker price of $27 000.

The GNX and Grand National were limited by an electronic fuel cut-out to a top speed of 120 mph or less, far short of the 150 mph that could easily have been achieved without interference. The cut-off was in

1988 Buick Grand National

The Buick Grand National was so fast that a quick, tantalizing view of the rear end was all most would-be speed challengers were likely to see of it.

the interests of safety for a car that enjoyed none of the handling and high-speed stability of its sister Camaro/Firebirds. The expertise of Buick's suspension and chassis engineering development was directed entirely toward front-wheel drive models, with rear-drive models treated as technological orphans whose time had run out. The sophistication of the Buick street racer was all under the hood. Though the wapping price put it beyond consideration for the under-thirty buyer, the entire limited run of Grand Nationals quickly sold out to people who were apparently enjoying extended childhood, and coveted the mind-warping acceleration which was thought to be almost extinct.

While Detroit V8s held off the Last Hurrah of the big-inch engine, Japanese sports compacts were carving away at the performance-market pie with small, high-tech, high-output motors in a wide variety of sizes and shapes. With the upscale, up-market sports GTs came a wave of low-market mini-chargers with four-cylinder powerplants tricked out with double-overhead cams, quad-valve heads, turbochargers and even superchargers. The super-high-performance technology made pocket rockets at small-car prices. The Mitsubishi-built Dodge Colt Turbo challenged the Mustang GT and IROC Z at half or two-thirds the price. Nissan dropped the V6 from the 300ZX into the budget-priced 200SX, turning it into a mini-muscle car. Honda produced the lightweight two-door fastback CRX coupe which delivered sports car performance from a small, high-efficiency, high-output four-cylinder engine at a small-car price.

The numbers and integers of performance were shifting steadily, with acceleration times falling, top speeds rising and prices climbing steeply at the upper end of the market. Acceleration numbers that were fast in 1975 were slow by 1985. After a decade of stagnation in which domestic cars seemed mired by gas prices and mileage and emission regulations, Detroit was dealing out performance from the top of the deck. The Mustang convertible returned in 1984, followed by convertibles from Corvette, the Camaro/Firebird and Chrysler LeBaron. With continuous pressure from Japan, technology was evolving so fast anything seemed possible. Oil prices had stopped rising halfway through the eighties and began to drop, bringing gasoline pump prices below $1 a gallon by 1987, which was as low as the pre-embargo prices before 1973, when factored for inflation. The return of cheap gasoline was a key factor in the resurgence of performance, along with a belief that oil prices would remain low for the near future.

It was an era without limits on performance, and people were prepared to pay for it. Though bargain performance cars like the Mustang were popular, so was performance at prestige-car prices. For 1986, Ferrari ascended to the ultra-exotic price and perfor-mance level of the US market with the $120 000 Testarossa, leaving the $60 000 V8 Ferrari 308GTB and its successor the 328 to the lower performance terrain where they belonged. The all-new, US-legal, mid-engined 12-cylinder Testarossa claimed a top speed of 180 mph with a 5 second 0-to-60 time, which made it just about the fastest production car in the

1988 Porsche 911 Speedster
To recapture the romance of the 1955 Speedster, Porsche reintroduced the name and the style in a special-edition 911. A statement of luxury as much as performance, the 1988 version commanded a price almost 20 times as great as the 1956–7 Speedster.

Overleaf: 1987 Ferrari Testarossa
After suffering an image decline in the early 1980s, Ferrari retook the world performance superiority position with the fierce 12-cylinder Testarossa, named after a famed fifties racing Ferrari.

world. The Testarossa replaced the fake Daytona Spyder as the TV wheels of *Miami Vice* and quickly became part of the new American dream.

The Testarossa had plenty of competition. Porsche had brought the 911 Turbo back to the US market after a five-year absence in which it was only imported through the quasi-legal network of 'grey-market' import-com-pliance shops. But the 911 Turbo was no longer the street car King Kong it had been in the seventies. With a 4.6 second 0-to-60 time, the $60 000 911 Turbo could leave just about anything off the line, but the 157 mph top end was a weak number even in Porsche's own family, where the $65 000 V8 928S4 recorded 170 mph in stock trim on the Bonneville salt flats.

Not even the 928S4 was fast enough to catch the Ferrari Testarossa in top gear, which made Porsche the second-fastest production car in America for the first time since the early seventies. Customizers and engine specialists in Germany produced modified 911 Turbos good for over 180 mph, with acceleration to humble Testarossas and price tags to match. The $80 000 to $100 000 price tags were not enough to keep the hot-rod Porsches off American streets, and the radical wide-fendered 'Slopenose' Porsche challenged the Ferrari Testarossa for top performance-status wheels in the country.

Some buyers of these ultimate performance cars were the traditional owners of extravagance on wheels: the celebrities and rich enthusiasts. But the mega-buck imported performance cars of the eighties were prominent on city streets in areas noted for a flourishing street drug trade, where billions in cocaine dollars created a new, untitled class of millionaire who drove nothing but the best and the fastest.

The fastest was getting faster. The extreme speeds described by the Banzai Runners and Autobahn rodders had raised the sights of the serious street speed-freaks. and the 170 mph and 180 mph production sports cars inspired visions of higher speeds. The 200 mph street car became the fanatic's dream, and auto magazines charted the steady procession of over-180 mph specials from shops in Germany and the United States. The Kremer Brothers and the German company DP produced rocket-speed twin-turbo Porsches, while German tuner Willi Koenig produced twin-turbocharged Ferrari 308s and Testarossas.

But none of the after-market specials matched the excitement generated by the Stuttgart speciality engineering firm AMG with its four-door, five-passenger

1987 Porsche 928S4
The Porsche 928 dismayed long-time Porsche purists when it was introduced in 1978 with a sophisticated, water-cooled V8 mounted in front. But the 928, with its sleek luxury and quiet super car performance, developed its own followers. By 1987, the 928 powerplant was producing over 300hp from a 32-valve, double-overhead cam engine. The price had climbed to over $60 000 and the top speed was over 160 mph. The 928S4 is a heavier car than the nimble 911, but as a high-speed autobahn-burner, it is a perfect gentleman's express.

187 mph Mercedes-Benz sedan. The blitzkrieg Benz which AMG named 'Hammer' was the hot-rod of all time. Made in the classic American hot-rod tradition that produced the Pontiac GTO and so many other performance legends, the Hammer was a mid-size 300 sedan modified to accept a heavily modified V8 from the 560 series, Mercedes-Benz's largest car, in place of the 300's six-cylinder engine.

A stock 560-series V8 would have made the AMG 300 a rocket, but that would not have been enough. With the help of custom-built quad-valve heads and double-overhead cams, AMG raised the 560 V8 power rating from 260 to 375hp. The suspension was suitably beefed up to cope with the added power and the body streamlined with spoilers, side skirts and airdams for streamlining and air-flow management at over 150 mph, writing a new chapter in the book of hot-rodding. While the Pontiac GTO, the Shelby GT 350 and the Camaro Z28 were exceptional in rivalling Ferrari, Corvette and Porsche performance with a low-priced American sedan, the AMG 'Hammer' was a five-passenger sedan that could literally blow the fastest Porsche, Ferrari or Lamborghini sports car off the road. It also had a higher price-tag – $130 000 – than almost any car ever offered for sale.

The Hammer had blacked-out chrome trim and tinted windows in the Euro-monochrome manner, combining New Wave, New Age muscle car style with performance unprecedented for a street car. The timed 187 mph top speed effortlessly humbled the Testarossa's best number and absolutely overwhelmed the $120 000 Lamborghini Countach which, despite its jet-fighter shape, had never managed much over 170 mph against the clock. Nothing on wheels could approach the blistering performance with seating for five adults, deep pile carpet, polished mahogany dash and panelling, and full luxury stereo sound.

Nothing for sale to the public, that is. Big-dollar hot-rodding in the United States was keeping pace with the fastest, most exotic machines coming out of Europe in the form of twin-turbocharged GM V8s. California speed tycoon Andy Granatelli, the former Indianapolis racing car owner, hot-rodder and TV advertising salesman, built an 840hp twin-turbocharged Camaro Z28 that was driven on the street and timed on the dry lakes at over 230 mph. Granatelli also had an 800hp street-legal Chevrolet Caprice four-door sedan with white vinyl roof that was timed at 219 mph. Both cars had stereo sound systems, electric windows, air-conditioning and power seats.

Granatelli's cars were built for the same reason hot-rods were always built – to outperform the fastest and most expensive cars on the road, which meant Ferraris, Porsches, Lamborghinis and hot-rod Mercedes-Benzes. Other twin-turbo V8 hot-rods gained membership in the over-200 mph club, including a Camaro, a Firebird Trans-Am and several Corvettes. A twin-turbocharged street-licensed Porsche Turbo Carrera built by Motorsport Design of Scottsdale, Arizona, cracked the 200 mph barrier for the 911 Turbo.

All these super hot-rods cost well over $100 000, but others followed which would go almost as fast for much less money. A new-generation super-Corvette

1987 Mercedes-Benz 320 E AMG
Hot-rodding climbed up the economic curve in the 1980s, with customizing and engine-tweaking being done to the most expensive prestige cars. This Mercedes-Benz features the custom aerodynamic body aids designed by the Stuttgart firm AMG, with engine performance modifications as well.

was announced for 1989 or 1990 as a $50 000 car with a top speed of at least 170 mph, with 200 mph rumoured for the not-too-distant future. Anti-skid brakes, four-wheel drive, active suspension and four-wheel steering were all market realities in the late eighties, along with horsepower-to-weight ratios higher than ever before. While Detroit continued to have difficulty competing with the down-size status cars from Germany, Sweden and Japan, American cars had a better grip on the performance market at the end of the eighties than at any time since the late fifties.

Japanese cars moved from the lower and middle positions to the top of the American market with the

1987 Mercedes-Benz 320 E AMG

AMG, like the Porsche hot-rodding shops Kremer and B & B, developed street-fighting supercars out of nearly every car in the Mercedes-Benz model line; from snarling, high-powered versions of the 190 four-cylinder to the staggering performance cars powered with the 5.6 litre V8. The style of the body modifications, usually painted in one colour with matching wheel covers, became a popular look in America and elsewhere.

engineering as offered by both the MK VII LSC and the 1988 Continental, Cadillac made a desperate move up-market to challenge the Mercedes-Benz 560SL with a two-door sports convertible named Allante. Attractively, if not imaginatively styled by Pininfarina, the Allante was woefully underpowered by an anaemic V6 and approached the 560SL only with its $55 000 price. Automotive enthusiast magazines were more than generous in making light of the Allante's yawing technological shortcomings but buyers were not, and Cadillac failed to meet even the minuscule target of a few thousand sales.

The American success of the Acura Legend, a sophisticated, moderate-priced luxury car from a Japanese economy-car maker, and the failure of an ill-conceived, overpriced Cadillac suggests a maturing in at least one segment of American auto-buying taste. The thriving sales of the high-tech Legend, with comparable cars on the way from other Japanese makers, spelt a smaller market share for US car-makers, but it also stood to improve the quality of cars on US streets.

The second half of the eighties encompassed and replayed every trend and phase of American automotive

V6-powered Acura Legend built by Honda. The Legend two-door coupe offered the substance of the BMW 635 image at $25 000, two-thirds the BMW price. As an all-new car for 1986, the Legend coupe was also a fashion-forward design considerably more contemporary than the ageing BMW 635. And the smooth, understressed Acura single-overhead-camshaft V6 was a more sophisticated engine than the BMW in-line six. The Acura Legend was a total success as a low-priced entry in the luxury sports sedan market that Cadillac was futilely trying to defend against Mercedes-Benz, BMW and almost everyone else except Chrysler. Hopelessly behind Lincoln in styling, performance and

1988 BMW 750iL
With the 750iL, BMW made it effortlessly to the top of the luxury-performance class. It had the smoothness of V12 power setting with none of the disadvantages of turbocharging or the high-strung characteristics of racing-tuned engines used in the performance versions of other luxury cars.

history. It was a time of explosive innovation and rapid market expansion with more types of cars available in more price ranges than ever before. It was also the time of the comeback, with the seeming return of every type of car, every model and every fad that had ever been popular. Small-engined small cars, big-engined small cars, small-engined big cars, big-engined big cars, good cars, bad cars, great cars, silly cars, cheap cars, fast cars and cars worth a king's ransom were all on the street and most were on the market. Sixties cars were back. Fifties cars were back. In another year or two, seventies cars would be back. The auto industry had changed not in excluding any kind of car or engineering, but by evolving, continually adding interlocking pieces of technology and market strategy for almost every taste and price range.

Hot-rodding was also back full-strength in an eighties revival of southern California street racing and cruising. It was a partial replay of the early fifties with cruise nights at drive-ins outside Los Angeles and street racers re-enacting the history of American hot-rodding. The revival brought back new versions of the early street rods, with both original and replica versions of 1932 Ford roadsters, Bucket Ts, Model As, 1934 Ford coupes, 1932 five-window coupes and other pre-war Fords favoured by hot-rodders then and now. Many of the new-wave hot-rods were brand-new imitations of thirties rods built from replica bodies available for most popular vintage hot-rod years. Most of the new wave of hot-rodding with old cars was done by men well into grown-up age who missed out on hot-rodding in their youth. Instead of resourceful garage mechanics and post-teens who were good at metal-work in school, $30 000 thirties hot-rods were built by men with enough money to recreate the dream car they could neither build nor buy as teenagers.

As the end of the eighties approached, the sweeping predictions made in the seventies were more distant from reality than ever. The American V8 was alive and well. Performance cars were faster than ever before. Sports cars were sportier. Taste and economic pressure had not down-sized cars into sub-compacts and mini-cars. Four-cylinder and six-cylinder engines were challenging V8 performance but not V8 sales appeal. European car-makers were making bigger, more powerful engines to keep ahead of the Japanese, and the Japanese were making bigger, more powerful engines to pursue the German, Swedish, Italian, British and American cars. The top line of Mercedes-Benz V8 models were all capable of close to 150 mph and

BMW raised the ante on Mercedes for 1988 with the 160 mph V12 750 sedan. Jaguar continued to rebuild a sodden prestige-performance image with the XJ6 and the XJ-S being taken seriously in the performance-luxury car marketplace alongside BMW, Porsche and Mercedes-Benz.

The long-term effect of the gasoline crunches of the seventies was a full-scale acceleration of technological progress that compressed several generations of engineering evolution into one decade. The mushrooming technology development war showed no signs of slowing, with notable advances in driving safety achieved with greater controllability, stability and stopping ability. Crash survivability, thanks to better seat belts and construction techniques, raised the odds of surviving a serious accident to an all-time high. Unfortunately, bad driving habits, chronic and widespread drunken driving, possibly aggravated by the climbing performance levels of modern cars, kept the death rate from automobile accidents catastrophically

Left: 1988 BMW 750iL
Above: 1985 Jaguar
XJ-S HE
Jaguar entered the eighties with a prestige image despite a stigma of unreliability earned by a series of unsuccessful sedans. Jaguar's fortunes in the US changed with the luxury-sport XJ6 and the 12-cylinder XJ-S two-door coupes. The XJ-S emphasizes comfort over performance, with the unfortunate marriage of a turbine-smooth V12 and a mushy three-speed hydromatic transmission by General Motors. But the price, sumptuous lines and luxury ambience helped make Jaguar a new prestige car in America.

high. Though the fatality rate in the United States did not rise perceptibly through the seventies and eighties, it remained in the low 40 000s annually. In other words, just under the total death toll of American servicemen in the Vietnam War was killed in highway accidents every year.

Towards the end of the eighties, the American dream on wheels was much what it had been in 1950, when almost every American dreamed of a powerful, shiny new car. The difference was that the dream car of the eighties needed high technology for a technology-conscious society. Brand-name loyalty had vanished as a market force, and little could be taken for granted in the automotive world. Boundaries and limits on performance, luxury, technology and driving pleasure which had closed in on the seventies were gone. The dream of the car as the symbol of the good life was alive and well on the American street, but it was unlikely that Detroit would ever regain the monopoly it had enjoyed back in the fifties.

CHRONOLOGY

1948: Cadillac and Oldsmobile introduce the overhead-valve V8. Studebaker reaches 4 per cent of the market. Hydramatic transmissions introduced for Cadillac, Oldsmobile and Pontiac. Hot Rod Magazine founded.

1949: Chevrolet breaks the million sales mark. GM profits reach $656 million.

1950: Ford overtakes Chrysler's sales and holds second place to GM. The Bel Air hardtop is introduced with Powerglide automatic transmission. Chevrolet is the number one selling car with 1.5 million sales. The Santa Ana drag strip opens in California.

1951: Chrysler introduces power steering. The National Hot-Rod Association is born.

1952: US Army General Dwight D. Eisenhower is elected President. The all-new styled Lincoln Capri V8 sweeps the Mexican road race, taking first, second, third and fourth places. Hudson Hornet wins 27 NASCAR races.

1953: Chrysler introduces the overhead-valve V8. Buick introduces the 322 cubic-inch OHV V8. Chevrolet brings out the six-cylinder, plastic-bodied Corvette. Cadillac's Eldorado convertible debuts. The Korean War ends. Lincoln sweeps the Mexican road race, again winning first, second, third and fourth places.

1954: GM builds its 50-millionth car, with the Cadillac V8 rated at 230hp. Ford produces the overhead-valve V8. Tubeless tyres offered on all new American cars. Chrysler averages 118 mph for 24 hours. Hudson Hornet wins 22 of 37 Grand National races on the NASCAR circuit.

1955: Lion's drag strip opens in Long Beach, California. Chevrolet's 265 cubic-inch V8 is introduced; production reaches a record 1.7 million. Cadillac sales reach a new high of 141 000. The Corvette V8 is introduced. The Chrysler 300 debuts with a 300hp hemi-head engine, and wins the NASCAR racing championship. Ford introduces the Thunderbird. The movies *Blackboard Jungle* and *Rebel Without a Cause* are released. *Rebel's* star, James Dean, dies 9–30–55. GM's after-tax profit exceeds $1 billion.

1956: Eisenhower wins a second term at the White House. Ford introduces the 312 cubic-inch V8. The Plymouth Fury debuts with a 303 cubic-inch V8. Lincoln Continental Mark II debuts. A Chrysler 300B sets the world's passenger-car speed record of over 139 mph at Daytona Speedway. There are now 55 million autos on America's roads. The Federal-Aid Highway Act is passed authorizing a national toll-free interstate highways system. A Chrysler 300 sets speed records at Daytona.

1957: Chevrolet's V8 is enlarged to 283 cubic inches, with fuel-injection available. Elvis Presley stars in the movie *Jailhouse Rock*. Ford dominates the NASCAR racing circuit, builds the 3-millionth Mercury, and introduces the Edsel. GM agrees to stop factory racing. American Motors discontinues the Hudson Hornet and Nash. Chrysler produces its 10-millionth Plymouth.

1958: Detroit auto-makers cease factory racing activities. The Chevrolet Impala debuts. Packard ceases production. Chrysler builds its 25-millionth car. A Pontiac Tri-Power Bonneville convertible is chosen as the pace car for the Indy 500. Ford introduces the 352 cubic-inch V8; Thunderbird becomes a four-seater. Imported car sales reach 385 000 units.

1959: There are now over 3,250 miles of limited access tollways in 21 states. American car-makers are caught in frenzy of ugly styling, with horizontal fins featured on the tails of most models. Small cars reach 18.4 per cent of the market share. California passes the first exhaust emissions law.

1960: John F. Kennedy is elected President. US has 3,841 shopping centres doing $35 billion annual business. A census reveals that four out of five American households has a car, with one out of five households owning two cars. American Motors sells 485 000 Ramblers, knocking Plymouth out of third place in America's car sales. Pontiac wins the NHRA Stock Eliminator title. Chevrolet's Corvair, Ford's Falcon and Plymouth's Valiant debut as American compact economy cars. The Edsel is discontinued. Chrysler drops the De Soto. A Chrysler 300F wins the Daytona flying mile with a speed of 145 mph. Total US car sales stand at 6.67 million.

1961: The Buick special compact is introduced. A Chrysler Newport wins the Mobil Economy Run with an average fuel economy of below 20 mpg.

1962: The Chevy II compact is introduced. The Ford Fairlane intermediate debuts. Former vice president Richard Nixon loses the race for governorship of California.

1963: Buick Riviera, a high-point in US auto design, debuts. The Corvette Sting Ray debuts with a 327 cubic-inch V8. The Shelby AC Cobra sets world performance records and wins a national road-racing championship. A Chrysler 300 convertible paces the Indy 500. President John F. Kennedy is assassinated in Dallas.

1964: Lyndon Johnson is re-elected President. Ford's Mustang debuts and achieves a record 500 000 sales in 18 months. An AC Cobra wins the US National Road-Racing Championship. The Pontiac GTO debuts. Front seatbelts become standard in US cars.

1965: Corvette gets a 396 cubic-inch engine option and four-wheel disc brakes. The Porsche six-cylinder 911 debuts. US auto sales hit a peak of 9.5 million. Ralph Nader publishes *Unsafe at Any Speed*, which indicts Corvair as a safety hazard. The US Congress passes the Air Pollution and Control Act, making exhaust emisision control devices mandatory on 1968 models. Ford produces Shelby's GT-350 Mustang. Jimmy Clark wins the Indy 500 in a rear-engined Lotus-Ford, ending decades of domination by American Offenhauser roadsters.

1966: Chevrolet's Z28 high-performance Camaro debuts. Pontiac gets a 400 cubic-inch V8. An AC Cobra wins the World Championship of sports-car racing. Corvette gets a 427 cubic-inch V8. Pontiac builds 96 946 GTOs. The US Congress passes the Highway Safety Act. Former movie actor turned TV host Ronald Reagan is elected governor of California.

1967: The BMW 2002 becomes a cult performance car. Chevrolet introduces the Camaro, Pontiac introduces the Firebird. Cadillac introduces the radical new front-wheel-drive V8-powered Eldorado, Oldsmobile introduces the front-wheel-drive Toronado.

1968: Richard Nixon is elected President. Imported cars reach a 10 per cent share of the market. The Steve McQueen movie *Bullitt* is released featuring the most exciting car chase ever filmed.

1969: Corvair production is discontinued. The movie *Easy Rider* is released. US troop strength in Vietnam reaches 550 000.

1970: Ford produces the Boss 302 Mustang. Corvette's engine is enlarged to 454 cubic inches. Congress passes the Federal Clean Air Act, intended to reduce auto emission pollutants by 90 per cent in six years. The Ferrari Daytona V12 establishes an unofficial claim to being world's fastest production sports car with a timed top speed of 170 mph. The Datsun 240Z debuts as the new sports car for the American market. Chevrolet introduces the Vega. Ford introduces the Pinto and Chrysler introduces its Omni sub-compact economy cars. Chevrolet also introduces the Monte Carlo. Janis Joplin records *Lord, won't you buy me a Mercedes-Benz?* on her last album. With 50 million cars on the road, a national census shows that three out of four Americans use cars to get to work in California. Five out of six commuters travel to and from work alone. Two out of five people living below the poverty line own cars. Cadillac debuts the world's biggest passenger car engine with the 500 cubic-inch Eldorado, and sells a record 239 000 cars. Ronald Reagan is re-elected governor of California.

1971: The movie *Vanishing Point* is released.

1972: Nixon is re-elected President, and presents a Fleetwood Eldorado coupe as a gift to Leonid Brezhnev. Burglary of Democratic National Headquarters in Watergate Hotel discovered.

1973: GM cars average less than 12 mpg fuel economy. A Cadillac Eldorado convertible is chosen as the Indiannapolis 500 pace car. The Vietnam War ends. The Arab oil embargo quadruples gasoline prices in the US and causes a fuel-crisis mentality. VW passes the Ford Model T production-longevity record with the Beetle. America's auto production of 11.4 million units is an all-time record. The movie *American Graffiti* is released.

1974: Facing certain impeachment by the US House of Representatives, President Nixon resigns and is immediately pardoned by Gerald Ford, who assumes the Presidency. A 55 mph national speed limit is imposed to save fuel.

1975: Chevrolet discontinues the 454 cubic-inch Corvette engine. Cadillac introduces the down-size front-wheel-drive Seville. US car sales are 38 per cent below the 1973 total, with more than 250 000 auto workers unemployed. Chrysler, whose losses stand at $259.5 million, announces the end of the Imperial. There are now 106 million cars on the road in the US. The Toyota Corolla becomes the first Japanese best-selling car in the world. Ferrari introduces the mass-production V8 Ferrari 308GTB. Porsche introduces the Turbo Carrera. VW Rabbit debuts as the successor to the VW Beetle.

1976: Gerald Ford is defeated in his re-election bid by Democrat Jimmy Carter of Georgia. The last of a long line of Cadillac convertibles is produced. The Vega is discontinued. The rate of highway deaths stands at 3.4 per 100 million vehicle miles, the lowest since 1923.

1978: The second Arab oil embargo doubles gasoline prices again. Fired by Ford, Lee Iaccoca joins Chrysler. Mercedes-Benz introduces the new Turbodiesel 300SD. The full-size pick-up is now the second largest-selling vehicle in the US.

1979: Chrysler requests Federal bailout to stave off bankruptcy.

1980: Ronald Reagan is elected President. Chevrolet introduces the front-wheel-drive Citation; Chrysler introduces the K-car. Japan builds 7 million cars, overtaking the USA as the largest car producing nation in the world. Federal law specifies corporate average fuel economy per manufacturer, with graduated reduction in consumption by year.

1981: Delorean goes on sale in the US.

1982: Delorean goes out of business. Chrysler brings back the convertible. Chevrolet's S-10 and S-10 Blazer mid-size trucks debut.

1983: Chrysler repays government loan with interest totalling $1.2 billion, seven years early. GM introduces the mid-engined, plastic-bodied Pontiac Fiero. A GM-Toyota joint venture is launched in California. Cadillac reintroduces the convertible. An all-new Corvette is introduced early as a 1984 model to immediate success.

1984: Ronald Reagan is re-elected President.

1985: Target of corporate average fuel economy of 27.5 mpg. Chevrolet IROC Z28 debuts with a tuned-port injection 305 cubic-inch V8.

1986: The new Corvette convertible debuts, anti-skid brakes available on Corvette.

1987: BMW introduces the V12 750i. Ford's world-wide earnings surpass those of GM for the first time since 1924.

1988: GM records the largest operating losses in American corporate history. The Cadillac Allante two-seater is named Flop of the Year by *Automotive News*. Pontiac discontinues the Fiero. Porsche suffers severe sales drop in the US.

FURTHER READING

Burness, Tad, *American Car Spotter's Guide*
(Osceola, WI, Motorbooks International, 1978)

Gunnell, John, *Standard Catalog of American Cars*
(Iola, WI, Krause Publications, 1987)

Halberstam, David, *The Reckoning*
(New York, NY, William Morrow & Co. Inc., 1986)

Hine, Thomas, *Populuxe*
(New York, NY, Alfred A. Knopf Inc., 1986)

Huntington, Roger, *American Supercars*
(Tucson, AZ, HP Books)

Langworth, Richard M. and Norbye, Jan P.,
The Complete History of General Motors
(Skokie, IL, Publications International Ltd, 1986)

Petersen's History of Drag Racing
(Los Angeles, CA, Petersen Publishing Co., 1981)

Sears, Stephen W., *The Automobile in America*
(New York, NY, American Heritage Publishing
Co. Inc., 1977)

Sexton, Richard, *American Style*
(San Francisco, CA, Chronicle Books, 1987)

Silk, Gerald, *Automobile and Culture*
(New York, NY, Harry N. Abrams Inc., 1984)

INDEX

PICTURE ACKNOWLEDGEMENTS

The Chrysler Corporation, 159; CW Editorial, 151, 152; Mirco Decet, 153; The Roland Grant Archive, 31; Kobal Collection, 36 bottom, 65 right, 105 bottom, 119, 166; The National Motor Museum, Beaulieu, 14, 21B, 26, 27, 30, 46, 48 top, 59 top, 59 bottom, 66 top, 68 top, 75 top left, 75 top right, 83, 92, 105 top, 110, 110–111, 116, 118, 124 bottom, 135 top right, 137, 141, 148–9, 149, 156–7, 158, 160 top, 160 bottom, 161, 162–3, 188, 222–3, 224, 225, 228–9, 230, 231; Porsche, 134–5, 136, 221; Quadrant Picture Library, 138, 150, 189, 226–7, 227, Rex Features, 134, 169 bottom.

All special photography by Nicky Wright, with special thanks to the following:

Auburn Police Department
Dennis Schebig
Bob French
Chris Trexler
Richard Carpenter
Phil Roche
Fred Engle
Jim Wall
Mike Nichols
Gary Gradat
Richard Hull
Allen County Motors
Larry Vielkin
H. J. Sanders
Nick Selsar
Tyrone Fritz
Chuck Edwards
Skip Campbell
Larry Brown
Art Saltzburg
Matt McBride
Frank Martino
Greg Perigo
Meredith Souers
Tom West
Rear View Mirror Museum
Becky Wright
Michelle Adam
Hilary Raab
Bobbie D'Ine Rodder
Merle Begley

Fort Wayne Police Department
Wayne Boyd
Ron & Robbie Miller
Bruce Myer
Jerry Ruskin
Dave Higby
Dianna & Larry Reisen
Mark Jones
Gene Duvall
Greg Patrick
Sam's Love Bug
Hugh Eshelman
Dennis Stoner
Elwin Young
Mike Crispin
Ford Motor Co.
Embassy Theatre
Derek's Motor Cars
Cinda Doubt
Andrew Kurtz/France Stone Co.
Gregg Munro
National Motor Museum
Paul Saverteig
Unique Color Lab
Burt Carlson & Friends
Mr. & Mrs. Ralph Wilson
Denny McKrill
Mike Cromer
Randell Reubarger
O'Daniels Oldsmobile
Roy & Barb Hathaway